Feng Shui ALMANAC 2000

Gary Quelch

郭皆利

foulsham

LONDON • NEW YORK • TORONTO • SYDNEY

foulsham

The Publishing House, Bennetts Close,
Cippenham, Slough, Berkshire, SL1 5AP, England

ISBN 0-572-02550-5

Printed in Great Britain by Cox & Wyman Ltd, Reading.

Contents

Dedication

I would like to dedicate this book to all my family, friends and loved ones who have supported and encouraged me over the years and who have provided me with the inspiration to put many of my ideas into practice. To my mother, my two sons, Ian and Oliver, and Stephanie, who has done such a wonderful job, a very big thank you.

I would also like to thank everyone at Foulsham, especially Wendy Hobson who showed considerable patience while waiting for the completed manuscript.

Finally, I would also like to mention Om Prakash, my grandmother Constance Newsham, and Camden the dog, who are all safe and well and who continue to watch over me.

Acknowledgements

This book would not have been possible without the work of others and I would like to express my gratitude and admiration to Martin Palmer, Mak Hin Chung, Kwok Man Ho and Angela Smith for their work on the T'ung Shu, published in 1986. Their book, *T'ung Shu, the Ancient Chinese Almanac*, remains the only book ever written in English on this subject and it has been a valuable source of inspiration.

I would also like to acknowledge the work of Derek Walters and in particular his book entitled *Chinese Astrology*, which was first published in 1987 and without which this book would not have been possible. This is still the only work written in English that deals with classical Chinese astrology, much of which he has translated from the original Chinese text. I was very fortunate to have had the opportunity of studying under the guidance of Derek, who inspired me to make the transition from studying Chinese medicine and nutrition, to feng shui and Chinese astrology.

Finally, I would like to acknowledge the work of Arthur Smith, who devoted much of his life to the study of Chinese philosophy, proverbs and sayings, and who in 1888 paved the way so that others, like myself, could follow behind.

Foreword

My fascination with the East first began over 25 years ago with an overland trip to India. I was very fortunate to meet a Swami, an Indian holy man, by the name of Om Prakash, who lived in the village of Mehrauli on the outskirts of New Delhi and who, quite simply, changed my life.

Over a period of nearly 15 years he taught me so much – a great deal of which I am only now really beginning to understand.

One of his favourite sayings was 'One day sure, all material finish, no problem' and this was his way of explaining that in order to come to terms with life, we must first come to terms with death. One day I pointed to a huge stone boulder and I said to Om, 'One day sure, this material finish', to which Om replied, 'Sure making'. I thought about this for a while and then I said, 'After this stone material finish, what making?'. He burst out laughing and looked at me as though he couldn't believe what I had said. 'After this material finish,' he said, 'this dust making and after dust making, wind coming and dust upside going.' As he said this he blew into his hand and then he said, hardly able to contain himself, 'And after rain coming, new material making.'

It has taken me years to realise that it really is that simple and that there are no such things as chaos, random incidents or coincidence, only sequences that we are unable to decipher or identify. Everything is linked to a cycle which, in turn, is part of another cycle and this is what links us with nature and the rest of the cosmos.

The Chinese calendar has not only been in use for 5,000 years, but it is unique because, unlike the Western concept of time which we express in numerical terms, the Chinese calendar expresses time in terms of elements, representing natural energy cycles in nature. It also incorporates lunar cycles and solar cycles as a means of expressing the energy created by the interaction of yin with yang – the primordial, complementary yet opposing forces of energy in the universe.

I have written this book to encourage everyone to use these natural energy cycles to 'go with the flow'. Feng shui has now become very popular and many people are becoming aware that the way we organise our space influences our lives. The next step is to realise that our space is already linked with our time, and for us to achieve real harmony, our calculations must include both time and space. Perhaps that was what they had in mind when they coined the phrase 'There is a time and a place for everything'.

Introduction

The Reverend Ernest J. Eitel's book, *Feng Shui, the Science of Sacred Landscape in Old China,* was first published in 1873. Working as a missionary in China for the London Missionary Society, he set out to document and record various aspects of Chinese culture. He was responsible for writing some of the earliest books in English on Buddhism and he is regarded by many as the first European authority on feng shui.

As a man of the cloth, he had a reverence for all forms of life but he was extremely surprised to discover that the Chinese shuddered at the thought of dissection, even for medical or scientific purposes. On visiting a medical college, he saw a group of students observing a frog, which seemed quite happy, hopping around its cage. He was told that they were studying the respiratory organs of the frog. Ernest told his guide that in Western science, this could only be achieved by dissection, examination and analysis. Ernest was shocked when his guide told him that they would never do such a thing and that Chinese science was based purely on observation.

He discovered that in China they looked at the stars but did not feel the need to invent instruments to help them, they analysed substances without the use of chemicals and they studied nature without the need for dissection. This impressed him above all else and he stressed his unhappiness at the Western approach to science, which feels the need to take everything apart, in order to discover how they work. The simplicity of the Chinese view is often confused with a childlike naivety, but as we become more educated and our technology more advanced, we are beginning to realise that in some ways, the ancient traditions were even more sophisticated than we are now.

The Chinese calendar has been in use for nearly 5,000 years and was devised using the same principles of observation that are still applied today. The ancient Chinese studied Earth as well as Heaven and everything they observed, they wrote down. This resulted in expressing time in terms of natural elements by identifying patterns and sequences of plant and animal behaviour, lunar and solar cycles and other natural phenomena. These were first used to identify the seasons, enabling farmers to obtain information for sowing, planting and harvesting, and this ancient system was known as the farmers' calendar and, like its Western equivalent, it was based on solar cycles.

Today, the Chinese calendar is based on lunar cycles with each year and each month beginning with the New Moon, although it still incorporates the original solar calendar to determine the seasons by solar cycles. These are known as the Joints and Breaths or the 24 Solar Chi and they play an important role in determining the movement of the seasons and other energy cycles.

The Chinese calendar also uses a system known as Heavenly Stems and Earthly Branches as a means of expressing the year, the month, the day and even the hour. 1999 is the year of the Earth Rabbit, the Earth being the Stem of the year and the Rabbit representing the Branch, and, by using the Chinese calendar, we are able to convert a Western date into the following breakdown: the hour of the Fire Horse, on the day of the Water Dragon, during the month of the Water Rooster, in the year of the Earth Rabbit. These pairs of characters are known as pillars – the hour pillar, day pillar, month pillar and year pillar – and this system is also used in a traditional form of Chinese astrology known as Fate Calculation or Pillars of Destiny.

The T'ung Shu Almanac has been in continuous print for more than 1,200 years, dating back to the T'ang Dynasty, when the first copy was always presented to the Emperor. It is read by millions of Chinese people every year, all over the world, and it offers practical advice on a whole range of issues concerning the home, the family, business and health. It contains information on astrology and feng shui and even advice for newly weds, although much of it is repeated every year. Many traditional homes keep a copy for good luck and it is usually allocated a very auspicious place within the home.

At the back of the T'ung Shu Almanac, there is a daily calendar that is based on the Chinese calendar but offers additional information for each day of the coming year and this information is based on a number of factors.

The first is the Stem and Branch of the day, which is taken from the calendar. In addition to this, the Essence – or as the Tibetans call it, the Body – is also taken into account. This is the element that is produced by the interaction between the Stem and the Branch.

This is one of the deeper aspects of Chinese metaphysics because there are fundamental reasons why combinations produce specific essences. The important thing is to try to be aware of how the benefits and disadvantages that the Essence of the day affect what we do. For example, if it is a day of potential conflict and the Essence of the day is Fire, any conflict that may arise will be made even worse by the addition of the Fire element.

Another two important factors are the 28 Constellations, which are known as the Lunar Mansions since they refer to lunar cycles, and a series of 12 indicators for the day known as Respected Master T'ung's method of Calculating Days or Clothes Cutting Days, and these represent the solar aspect of the day, since their sequence is linked with the solar cycles.

This results in a unique, integrated system incorporating the movements of Heaven and Earth, the Sun and the Moon and, from this, certain activities are regarded as being favourable or not. It is important to stress that this information applies to everyone and it is not based on personal astrology but on the natural cycles of nature which affect everyone. The Chinese believe that by following the flow of the Almanac it is easier to be in harmony with their environment, their loved ones and, not least, with themselves.

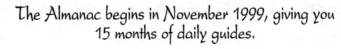

The Almanac begins in November 1999, giving you
15 months of daily guides.

Insight into the Coming Year: The Metal Dragon

A glance at the T'ung Shu Almanac for the year 2000 reveals the Ox boy standing to the right of the Ox, which signifies that the year begins after the Li Chun Spring festival. This denotes that this year is regarded as a 'blind' year, because it begins without the blessing of Spring. To make things worse, this year is a 'double-blind' year because it ends before the next Li Chun, which means, in effect, a year without a Spring festival.

Since Spring usually leads the way into the year, this may result in many people losing their focus, becoming lost and confused. As a result, it is very important to retain a sense of purpose and direction this year and there is no better way to do that than to be in touch with the seasons, nature's natural cycles. This is especially true in a double-blind year, because without the light of Spring to light the way, in the form of the Li Chun Spring festival, these are the only markers available to guide us through the coming year.

We can also see that the Ox Boy is not wearing his hat, which means that he is not expecting a heatwave, and as a result there appears to be little prospect of a hot Summer. On top of that, he is also wearing his shoes, from which we can deduce that he is expecting heavy rain this year, so, on the whole, the weather prospects don't look very good.

The Lo Shu Square

In the feng shui section of the Almanac, usually at the front of the book, the Lo Shu magic square is given, with all the relevant information for feng shui masters to determine auspicious directions for the coming year. These apply to burial sites as well as homes and businesses, and they form the basis of many different styles of what is known as flying star feng shui or Fei Xin.

Each year is said to be governed by a Ruling Star, which is associated with one of the nine numbers of the magic square. In an arrangement which is known as the Later Heaven Sequence, the numbers are arranged in such a way that all the lines add up to 15 by placing the number 5 in the centre.

4	9	2
3	5	7
8	1	6

By placing south at the top and north at the bottom – which is the customary Chinese way of representing the compass points – we can now use this to determine what direction any given star is said to represent. In this case, south is represented by 9, west by 7, and so on.

Although the Later Heaven arrangement of the Lo Shu is a standard, the pattern of the numbers is said to change every year, as the stars fly around the square in a given sequence according to the Ruling Star for that year.

The T'ung Shu Almanac reminds us that the year 2000 is a number nine year and so nine is the Ruling Star and is therefore placed in the centre. The other stars are placed accordingly, following a strict sequence.

This is the Lo Shu map for the coming year, but it is only really the basis of many other calculations that feng shui masters use in order to determine the fortunes of a building. This is because, in addition to the Ruling Star allocated to each year, each cycle of 20 years is also said to be under the influence of one of the Nine Stars. This fact is often used as the basis on which to determine the so-called birth chart of a building. It is important therefore to keep in mind that this is only general information, but it does form the very basis of flying star feng shui and it is therefore important to understand the concept and its application before you can move on to consider the subject in more depth.

9	5	7
8	1	3
4	6	2

Lo Shu Chart for the Year 1999

8	4	6
7	9	2
3	5	1

Lo Shu Chart for the Year 2000

In flying star feng shui, different numbers and directions are considered lucky or unlucky for specific areas of life. The stars are also associated with colours, sharing yellow, green, black, purple and white between the nine stars.

The most unlucky number is five, the yellow star. For 2000, this is in the north, moving from the south where it was situated in 1999. This star is often associated with illness and disaster and is the one that should be avoided the most. If you are ill, avoid this as your facing direction.

The other unlucky number is two, the black star, which is again associated with illness. This has moved from the north-west to the west and this is another area or direction to avoid.

The only other star which is generally considered to be inauspicious is the number three, the jade star, which is associated with conflict. This has moved from the west, where it was in 1999, to the north-east.

The auspicious number eight, the white star, often associated with generating wealth, has moved from its 1999 position in the east, to the south-east. This is a good opportunity to try to improve your finances by making sure that the areas within your home and business associated with the south-east are kept free of clutter to allow the favourable influence to penetrate your life.

The other auspicious star associated with wealth and money, number six, the white star, has moved from the north to the south-west and, as before, this area also needs particular attention in order to benefit from the positive aspects of the coming year.

For those at university or engaged in study, the auspicious number four, the green star, which many associate with learning and academic pursuits, has moved from the north-east to the south.

In addition to their positions for the year, the flying stars also move around in the same sequence on a month-to-month basis. More information regarding the other stars and how they move in this way can be found in the section on flying stars, starting on page 165.

The Grand Duke in the Area of the Dragon

The Grand Duke, the name by which the Chinese refer to Jupiter, is considered to be in the area of the Dragon for the coming year, which is roughly in between east and south-east. According to traditional Chinese belief, the Grand Duke should never be confronted and there are numerous tales in the Chinese classics relating to defeats of large armies at the hands of a force which, although much smaller, had the support of the Grand Duke. In feng shui terms, this area should be left alone and on no account should any building work take place here, because it would be considered as 'disturbing the Grand Duke', something which should always be avoided.

The Five Seasons

It is important to remember that the first rule in 'going with the flow' is to be in harmony with the seasons themselves and to use the different energies associated with each season to your advantage. Do the things pertaining to the Spring during the Spring and not during the Summer. If you plan your year according to these ancient traditions, you will have nature's natural energy cycles working for you and not against you, helping you to enrich not only your own life, but also the lives of those around you.

Spring: The Wood Element February 4–May 5

The three months associated with Spring are February, March and April. The element of Spring is Wood, associated with new beginnings, generative growth and new chi energy, which rejuvenates and stimulates plants, animals and humans, as well as ideas and aspirations. The Spring equinox is a time when day equals night, but after this, the yang energy begins to accelerate and take over. During this time, it is good to be very active and to put into motion the things that you want to achieve this year. This is the time to plant seeds, open up new beginnings and plan ahead.

Many people are still in their Winter mode long after Christmas, and this can often have a negative effect on the entire year, because what you achieve in the Spring influences what you can harvest in the Autumn. It is very important to keep this in mind and to make the most of the Spring energy, irrespective of the weather, because the more you sow, the more you can reap. When we begin to notice that buds are already appearing, this is nature's way of reminding us that Winter is over, even if there is snow on the ground.

Summer: The Fire Element May 5–August 6

The three months associated with Summer are May, June and July. The element of Summer is Fire, associated with brightness, warmth and a developing and prospering chi energy which makes things flourish and grow. At this time of the year, it is good to cultivate and develop ideas and projects that were started in the Spring and to use this expansive energy to enable these things to grow. The Summer solstice represents yang energy at its height and if the weather becomes too hot during this time of year, things can get out of hand, so the need for balance must be kept in mind. It is not surprising that hot, dry summers are often a prelude to civil unrest and when we are too hot tempered, things are more likely to escalate out of control. Summer should not be seen as a time to let off steam but a time when we should utilise our energy for cultivation, looking after those things that were started in the Spring and from which we will be looking to harvest come the Autumn.

Autumn: The Metal Element   August 7–November 6

The three months associated with Autumn are August, September and October. The element of Autumn is Metal, associated with rigidity, determination and a reforming chi energy that enables us to bring things to a conclusion and to harvest the fruits of our labours. During this time we have the Autumn equinox, when once again day is equal to night, but once this has passed, the yin energy begins to accelerate and exert its influence. At this time of year, it is important to use the remaining active chi to provide the will-power to complete the tasks that were begun in the Spring and developed during the Summer. This is the time to gather together our resources and to accumulate enough to see us through the Winter. It is a good time to get into a disciplined routine and to begin to store our resources. The Metal element is also associated with money and this is an excellent time of the year to attend to finances and to get them under control.

Winter: The Water Element   November 7–February 3

The three months associated with Winter are November, December and January. The element of Winter is Water, associated with retreating and returning chi energy, which enables us to nurture our vitality and to replenish our inner strength. This is the dormant period of the year when we should sleep longer, rest more and eat nourishing food. Many animals and plants use this time to hibernate and rest and we should try to follow their example. This period contains the Winter solstice, when yin energy reaches its peak and then begins its decline. It is always good to remember that once Christmas is here, the nights begin to get shorter and the days longer. The Water element is also associated with obstacles and emotions and it is important to balance out this yin energy in order to avoid becoming depressed and over-emotional. Balance is the key, and if you suffer during the dark, cold winter, then perhaps you should consider having your annual holiday at this time of year.

The Earth Season: The Earth Element   April 17– May 4, July 20– August 6, October 20–November 6, January 17–February 3

In China they call this period 'the four season' because it crops up four times a year at the end of each of the four usual seasons, and each time it arrives, it lasts for 18 days. This explains why four of the 12 Chinese animals are represented by the Earth element, because these also represent the last month in each of the four seasons. The Dragon is Spring Earth, the Sheep is Summer Earth, the Dog is Autumn Earth and the Ox is Winter Earth. The Earth element is associated with stability and grounding and this period provides a stabilising chi energy that enables us to make an adjustment and to steady ourselves before the next step.

Month 10

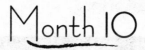

Monday November 8 – The Wood Rat – Essence of the day is Metal

Today's New Moon marks the beginning of the tenth lunar month of this year. It also coincides with the solar festival of Li Tung, which means the beginning of Winter and therefore marks the first day of the Winter season. We are now entering the Water period of the year and during this time the chi energy is returning and retreating and it is natural to begin to wind down and begin resting more to conserve energy. Many animals and plants hibernate in the winter, and in an ideal world we too would minimise our activity during the Winter. Unfortunately, of course, this is impossible for most people – unless you have won the Lottery. The important thing to remember is that it is vital during this period to eat more and sleep more and to try to conserve as much energy as possible, so remember the Chinese proverb that says:

 A man who runs too fast drops his rice bowl.

Tuesday November 9 – The Wood Ox – Essence of the day is Metal

If you have planned to move into a new home today, then you have made a fortunate choice because the Almanac supports this kind of activity. Important events in general are also very well favoured so if you are at work, today represents an opportunity to get the week off to a flying start. Not a day to spend on tedious, mundane, routine issues; this is a time to set your sights a little higher, because much can be accomplished today. If you are stuck at home and are tempted by some gardening work to alleviate the boredom, try to find something else to occupy your attention, because outdoor activities are not considered to be favourable today.

Wednesday November 10 – The Fire Tiger – Essence of the day is Fire

Variable fortune is in the energies today, so we will all have to learn to accept the yin with the yang. Gardening in general is not considered to be favourable, especially landscaping, but if you are planning to move into a new home today, things should go very smoothly because the portents are in your favour. For those staying at home, whether they are working, looking after the children or studying, it would be wise to spend a little time sitting quietly and thinking about future plans. Winter is a good time to nurture vitality and to replace the energy that has been used up during the course of the year. Contemplation and meditation are excellent ways to build up inner strength and personal energy and the T'ung Shu Almanac reminds us of that today.

FENG SHUI ALMANAC 2000

Thursday November 11 – The Fire Rabbit – Essence of the day is Fire

An active day that should be put to good use, so use this time to get things done. Industrious actions are rewarded today and this should provide us with the incentive to motivate ourselves and put things into action. It is surprising how much easier it is to accomplish this when we are in harmony with the natural energy cycles, so even if you don't feel like doing much, make an effort and you may well be pleasantly surprised. Feng shui water features in the garden are very well favoured today, because not only does Respected Master T'ung encourage the opening of wells, but the Constellation indicates that great riches will come in time to those who create new watercourses today.

Friday November 12 – The Earth Dragon – Essence of the day is Wood

If you are tempted to go to the bank and withdraw some of your savings, think again, because today is not a good time to do this. Travel and movement in general are also considered to be unfavourable, so it is a good day to stay in, whether at home or at work, and get down to the job in hand. If you are interested in divination of any kind and you have been thinking of having a tarot reading or your horoscope interpreted, then today would be a very good time to have this done, because one of the indications today is known as the Ghostly Carriage, when the spirit world is particularly active. But since we are also informed that the Emperor bestows his blessings, these forces can be harnessed for our benefit, at least for today.

Saturday November 13 – The Earth Snake – Essence of the day is Wood

A day of conflict and confrontation and a time when everyone should think very carefully before entering into arguments of any kind. *The Art of War*, a book by Sun Tzu, is an amazing example of the principles of yin and yang adapted in order to try to understand conflict by realising that the art of war is also the art of peace. In this book we are reminded that unless we know the disadvantages of using force, we cannot know the advantages, and this should be kept in mind today. The T'ung Shu predicts that harmful actions will result in sickness and ruin, and any short-term benefits that may be derived from using force today will pale in comparison to the retribution that will follow. Positive actions are the remedy, coupled with empathy and compassion, because a few kind words delivered in a positive, understanding way will perform miracles while anything else at all will only aggravate the situation. Go with the flow, or, as the Chinese proverb reminds us:

   Follow the square and comply with the round.

Sunday November 14 – The Metal Horse – Essence of the day is Earth

The saying 'If at first you don't succeed, try again' should be ignored today: the advice in the T'ung Shu Almanac is to walk away if things don't work. 'Be happy and drink wine' is the advice offered by Respected Master T'ung and if you have nothing better to do, then why not? The winter period is for taking it easy – or at least easier – and it is a time when we should nurture our vitality in preparation for the coming year. It is a time to rebuild our defences and to store our vital energy, so the best advice would be to eat, drink and be merry – after all, it takes less energy to smile than to frown, and good food and good wine are the perfect companions of good friends, so enjoy the day and encourage others to do the same.

Monday November 15 – The Metal Sheep – Essence of the day is Earth

With the right attitude and the correct conduct, much can be accomplished today and this is an excellent opportunity to get the week off to a good start. Business, commerce and industry can all flourish and so can relationships, resulting in happiness and harmony. The portents also favour those who are departing on long journeys, so anyone fortunate enough to be going on a winter holiday to some exotic location should feel very pleased with themselves. Clearly, activity is the key word of the day, so even if you are at work but you would rather be on vacation, don't allow negativity to ruin your day, because, with the right approach, today may well pave the way for a holiday of a lifetime at a later date.

Tuesday November 16 – The Water Monkey – Essence of the day is Metal

A good day for trading even if it means dipping into savings, because we are told that Heaven's treasures are received today and so we should 'open the granaries'. However, this should not be used as an excuse to fritter away hard-earned cash, but be seen as an opportunity to utilise your business skills. This is emphasised by the fact that celebrations in general are not considered to be very favourable, so keep in mind that the portents favour dedication and concentration rather than jubilation. Of course, the secret is to be happy in your work and if you go about your tasks in a happy and enthusiastic manner, Heaven is certain to bestow its blessings on your efforts.

Wednesday November 17 – The Water Rooster – Essence of the day is Metal

Another auspicious day and one of the portents is symbolised by the Celestial Carriage, which was traditionally associated with the transport of gifts for the Emperor and therefore with the arrival of wealth. The arts are also well favoured and those who paint, play music or practise any other creative activity should search for additional inspiration because it's out there somewhere. The Heavenly Doctor is also on duty today, attending to the Emperor of Heaven's messenger. He dispenses his healing powers to all who need him, so if you have been suffering recently, take heart, because things will begin to improve, and keep in mind the Chinese proverb that says:

 That which happens without man's doing is done by Heaven.

Thursday November 18 – The Wood Dog – Essence of the day is Fire

A conflict of interests today and as a result it may be difficult to know what to do. In this situation, the smart money would be to hedge one's bets and not do anything drastic. This is a day when everything is considered to be closed, so activity should be kept to a minimum. Paperwork and correspondence are fairly suitable, so, if there are any letters to attend to, today is an appropriate time to deal with them. The positive indications are new beginnings and, if this is coupled with the practical advice given by Respected Master T'ung, then we should focus on the networking aspects of the day. So check your e-mail and surf the Net because you will never know what is out there unless you go and find out. The indications are that any leads developed today will in time bring great benefits.

Friday November 19 – The Wood Pig – Essence of the day is Fire

Today should provide an active end to the week, especially if you are in business, because today is a good day for all types of trading. It would be wise to look at the accounts and to chase up anything that is outstanding, as well as paying any bills that are overdue. The Almanac advises against outside activities such as building, gardening and anything that requires heavy manual labour, so these should be avoided if possible. Shopping trips should also be avoided, unless they are for essential groceries or household items, because we are advised against the use of savings. Taking precautions is always the best course, so if you need to shop and you suffer from 'comfort shopping' – or 'displacement therapy', as a friend of mine referred to it – then leave the plastic at home.

Saturday November 20 – The Fire Rat – Essence of the day is Water

Not a fortunate day for a wedding, because the Almanac suggests that children born of a marriage today will be poor. Sporting activities are well favoured and so are matters relating to health, so whether you enjoy football, yoga, badminton or swimming, today is a very good day to make the effort. Feng shui remedies are also very well favoured, because today represents an opportunity to clear away negative energy and obstacles that prevent us from making progress. If you find yourself at home today, take a look around and see what you can do to create more space and to encourage new, fresh energy into your life. If you are looking to attract a new partner into your life, spend some time clearing away the influences of previous relationships, such as letters, photographs and reminders of things that are now in the past. Only by really letting go can we create the opportunity to grasp new opportunities, and by clearing out old cycles, we encourage new cycles to begin.

Sunday November 21 – The Fire Ox – Essence of the day is Water

A day that favours important issues and grand venues, so don't be intimidated if you are attending a big event, because it is definitely a case of 'the bigger the better'. This applies whether you are attending the event or working there, so it doesn't matter in what capacity you are involved – just enjoy it. One of the omens indicates health, wealth and happiness, especially relating to the home, so it is another good day for implementing feng shui remedies, although these should be confined to the inside of the home and should not include external remedies. If you find yourself moving into a new house today, then you are very fortunate because the Almanac predicts a bright future for those who find themselves in this position today.

Monday November 22 – The Earth Tiger – Essence of the day is Earth

Today is the day of the Full Moon and if you feel emotionally charged, try to mellow out and take things in your stride. Communication is the key today, symbolised by the element of Water, and since this is now the Winter, or Water, period of the year, it is more important than ever to use this valuable resource. Balance is the key in all areas today and any time spent in meditation and contemplation will pay dividends, especially when the Spring comes. This is, after all, a time to store and nurture our vital resources and a time to try to make life as easy as possible for ourselves. If this all sounds too simple, then consider the words of the ancient sage who said:

Words that are simple but far-reaching in meaning are good words.

Tuesday November 23 – The Earth Rabbit – Essence of the day is Earth

Today is the solar festival of Hsiao Hsueh, which means 'little snow', and, as the name suggests, this is a time when Winter really begins to make its mark and the Water element starts to influence the chi. The portents are very favourable today for all kinds of activities and everyone should try to make the most of these fortunate blessings. There are indications of hidden treasure, promotion and rich descendants from marriages, so it is clearly a very favourable time. Today is also the birthday of the goddess Wu-shan, considered to be a deity who looks after married couples, and on this day they give thanks to Wu-shan for their lives together. If you are in a happy relationship, spare a thought for Wu-shan today and thank her for your life with your partner.

Wednesday November 24 – The Metal Dragon – Essence of the day is Metal

With the exception of moving home and travelling, today is another auspicious day that should encourage everyone to keep themselves busy. The Almanac informs us that opening new doors today can double our fortune and with motivation like that, who could not resist reaching for the stars? If you wake up and look out of the window and it's cold and wet (or even worse), shake off those winter blues, have a hot shower and tuck into a hearty breakfast. With such a start, you can begin to plan out your strategy to make the most of the opportunities at your disposal, and with the right attitude and the right approach, success is there for the taking.

Thursday November 25 – The Metal Snake – Essence of the day is Metal

A day of conflict in more ways than one, because there is a real yin and yang feel to the day. On the one hand, arguments, confrontations and conflicts are indicated, and on the other hand, a stimulating, encouraging energy, denoting prosperity. Possibly a day when the right hand doesn't even know where the left hand is, let alone what it's doing, and the best advice would be to let it do what it wants. It would not be wise to challenge authority of any kind and if you find yourself on the receiving end of a parking ticket, don't get annoyed; take your medicine with a smile – after all, they are only doing their job. Keep in mind the Chinese proverb that says:

 When your work is done, then withdraw, because that is the way of Heaven.

Friday November 26 – The Water Horse – Essence of the day is Wood

One of the portents today is associated with the Ox Boy, who is forever separated from his lover, the Weaving Maiden, whom he is only allowed to meet for one day each year. This time he is coupled with another unfavourable portent, which only makes his depression worse. It is always difficult being separated from friends and loved ones but if you try to remain positive and think happy, warm thoughts, these are often transmitted to your partner, which frequently cheers them up. It is always good to remind ourselves that in every yin there is a yang, but you do have to look for it. One thing is certain, however: you will not find it by dwelling on negative aspects. If you are on your own, telephone a few friends and see what they are doing, put on your best smile and take yourself out and join in the fun – after all, it's Friday night.

Saturday November 27 – The Water Sheep – Essence of the day is Wood

Things have improved today and everyone should make the most of it. A day suitable for all types of activity, so keep busy, but, more importantly, keep out of other people's business. Outside activities are considered to be very favourable, so if you have an abundance of energy and you find yourself at home, then why not get out in the garden? There is always something to do there even in the Winter and, at the very least, you should make an effort to keep it clear and tidy. Bird feeders need to be filled, and encouraging birds to come into the garden is very good feng shui because it encourages new, fresh chi to enter the home. Nesting boxes are also very good and looking after wild birds is a wonderful way of repaying nature for her kindness to us.

 Men die for gain; birds perish because of a lack of food.

Sunday November 28 – The Wood Monkey – Essence of the day is Water

Today is not a good day for outside activities, so perhaps it would be wise to spend the day at home. Studying is very well favoured today and any form of education is considered to be auspicious, so anyone attending courses or workshops should receive additional inspiration. This applies equally to the teachers as well as the pupils, so this is a day when both parties should push themselves to the limit. The alternative to this is curling up in front of a warm fire and reading whatever takes your fancy, especially if you have been working all week and this is the first chance you have had to relax. It is Winter, after all, so there is every reason to conserve your energy.

Monday November 29 – The Wood Rooster – Essence of the day is Water

Conflicting energies again today, but if you try to avoid travel, especially by ship, then the good will outweigh the bad and that way we can all profit. Business dealings are very well favoured and today is a good day to get in touch with friends, family and loved ones, so why not take advantage of modern technology and telephone a few friends? The Essence of the day is Water, the season represents Water, and since Water is associated with communication there will obviously be benefits in going with the flow. The Heavenly Doctor is on call again today, attending as always to the Emperor of Heaven's messenger, and if you have been feeling below par recently, there is every indication that you will benefit from his visit.

Tuesday November 30 – The Fire Dog – Essence of the day is Earth

Many people may find themselves very confused today because the portents are certainly confusing. Everything looks so bleak, there is every reason not to bother getting out of bed and yet, in contrast, fortunate blessings are dropping from the sky. It's a question of take what comes and hope for the best, while at the same time being prepared for the worst. Whether you are at home or at work, the best advice would be to try to get into a routine as quickly as possible, focus on what you are doing and keep a low profile. Any fortunate blessings are certain to find you, no matter where you are, but if you keep yourself to yourself, you may well improve your chances of steering clear of any trouble that may arise. After all, as the Chinese say:

 If we want to cross the sea, we need the aid of a boat.

Wednesday December 1 – The Fire Pig – Essence of the day is Earth

A good day for trading and a good time to have a look at the accounts and see what is outstanding and deal with it. Heavy manual work is not particularly favourable, so try and keep to paperwork and dealing with enquiries or estimates. Shopping is also very well favoured but the T'ung Shu warns against the use of savings, so don't look out for bargains as an excuse to shop until you drop. Travel is also considered to be unsuitable today, so if this is unavoidable, then you would be wise to take the usual precautions. Allow plenty of time if you are using public transport, because there is every chance of congestion and delays. If you are driving, then exercise even more caution than usual.

Thursday December 2 – The Earth Rat – Essence of the day is Fire

This is another good day to clear out negative influences, whether they are emotional, spiritual or physical. Obstacles exist everywhere – we erect them for ourselves and sometimes they are built for us – but they all prevent us from moving on. These blockages exist in many forms, from negative ideas and misconceptions to rubbish and clutter. The fewer we have, the easier it is for us to operate. Not only are we able to flow better but beneficial energy can also circulate more easily, revitalising and inspiring us to greater things. Sports and therapies are also well favoured today, so if you feel like pampering yourself with a session of your favourite therapy after work, don't feel guilty – leave that to others and instead enjoy every minute.

Friday December 3 – The Earth Ox – Essence of the day is Fire

An excellent night for a party and the bigger it is, the better; so, if you are planning to have one and you are a little nervous, rest assured – you have selected a good night and no doubt it will go down with a bang. For those with more important matters to deal with first, it is a good day for meetings of any kind. So if you have an appointment to see the bank manager, the boss or even the Aga Khan, you should feel confident because the portents are very favourable. All you have to do is to put on your favourite outfit, wear your best smile and turn up on time, because if you are looking good and feeling good, you are certain to be at your best.

Saturday December 4 – The Metal Tiger – Essence of the day is Wood

Today is the Festival of the North Pole Star and anyone practising or studying Chinese astrology or feng shui should bear this in mind and light a candle or burn some incense in honour of the occasion. The Plough, or Great Bear, is the great clock in the sky which swings around according to the seasons while always pointing north to the Pole Star. It is the most important group of stars in the Heavens as far as the Chinese are concerned, because it is the home of the gods. This is therefore a day of celebration for all the occupants of Heaven and it would be appropriate to remember the words of Confucius, who said:

One who governs with morality is like the North Star, which holds its position while the other stars pay homage to it.

Sunday December 5 – The Metal Rabbit – Essence of the day is Wood

A fairly active day, although not all the activity is favourable and it would be wise to be fairly cautious. Squabbles should be avoided, especially domestic ones, because the T'ung Shu predicts that these will lead to unhappiness and regret, so this is a day when everyone at home should make an extra effort to be nice to each other. Diplomacy and tact are valuable attributes at the best of times, but even more so on days like this when restraint, empathy and understanding are what is required. Be happy, encourage others to be happy, and look on the bright side of life. Give thanks for what is good and try to improve what is not, because if we strive to make an effort, we encourage others to follow suit.

Monday December 6 – The Water Dragon – Essence of the day is Water

An auspicious day and one which may well bring some very nice surprises because one of the portents is symbolised by the net, indicating opportunities presenting themselves and things turning up unexpectedly. The Almanac advises against moving home today and travel is also not considered to be very favourable, so try to avoid this if possible and, if not, expect delays and cancellations, so allow plenty of time. Domestic activity is considered very appropriate and since there is an indication of things turning up unexpectedly, if you clear out the garage, the loft or the spare room, you may well come across a little treasure – so be careful what you throw away.

Tuesday December 7 – The Water Snake – Essence of the day is Water

Today is the solar festival of Ta Hsueh, which means 'great snow', and this marks the beginning of the second month of Winter. The Water element will now become very prominent and its influence will begin to have an effect on everything: plants, animals, ideas and relationships. It is good to remind ourselves that the nature of Water is returning and retreating, and at times like this it really pays to go with the flow. Things may look a little bleak for some people, but much of this is to do with the fact that there is no Moon and this tends to enhance negativity. Look forward to the New Moon tomorrow and see it as the beginning of another new cycle which can be as positive as you are prepared to make it. Let's face it, we bring many of our problems upon ourselves, but things don't have to be that way. We have the power to change our lives and we only have ourselves to blame if we don't want to use that power for the good.

Month 11

Wednesday December 8 – The Wood Horse – Essence of the day is Metal

Today is the day of the New Moon and the beginning of the eleventh lunar month for this year, according to the Chinese calendar. A difficult start to this month is indicated and one that may well result in conflict and arguments, so it would be wise to remember this today. New Moons are always associated with new energy and it would be unwise for anyone to taint this opportunity with negative, aggressive behaviour. Empathy and compassion are what is needed today and we should all try to develop these attributes within ourselves as well as encouraging them in others. A few kind words are often all that is needed to diffuse a difficult situation, and on days like this, it is the only remedy because anything else will only result in an escalating conflict. Respected Master T'ung reminds us today there are no winners, only losers, so keep in mind the following:

*Just as we take advantage of what is, so we should
recognise the usefulness of what is not.*

Thursday December 9 – The Wood Sheep – Essence of the day is Metal

A day of variable fortunes when many will no doubt feel frustrated and if that applies to you, the best course of action is to walk away from whatever it is that is causing it. Not a day to swim against the tide but a day to float down the river, because what works, works, and what doesn't, doesn't, and today, at least, there is not a lot that can be done to change that. The T'ung Shu advises us to be joyous and drink wine and if you find you are not having a good day, why not unwind with a glass or two with a few friends? Better still, why not combine this with a good meal? After all, there is no better company for wine than good food, good friends and pleasant conversation.

Friday December 10 – The Fire Monkey – Essence of the day is Fire

Another day of conflicting fortune when some may benefit enormously, while others may suffer a great deal, and if you want to play it safe, then keep busy and mind your own business. Everyone would do well to avoid any trickery today, even if it is harmless fun, because others may not take too kindly to this light-hearted approach. The best advice would be to direct your energy to matters relating to work and if you can do this, you are certain to improve your chances of success. With conflicting fortunes, the smart approach is to keep a low profile because favourable influences will find you if they really want to, while negative forces seem to influence almost everything they come across.

Saturday December 11 – The Fire Rooster – Essence of the day is Fire

Study and education are both highlighted but today is very auspicious for all kinds of activities and therefore a day not to be wasted. Trade in general is also considered to be very well favoured, so this is another day to keep busy and make the most of any opportunities that may come your way. Travel is not regarded as very suitable, so it would be wise to keep this in mind and if you do have to make a journey, allow plenty of time for delays, congestion and all the other negative aspects of modern travel. For those at home, try to keep yourselves busy, but resist the temptation to dig up the garden: outside activities are not considered to be favourable, so stay in and keep warm.

Sunday December 12 – The Earth Dog – Essence of the day is Wood

A day of rest and recuperation, which will be very welcome for those who have been suffering recently, and also a good time to sit back and recharge your batteries. If you have not been in touch with friends and family for a while, today is a good time to get out the address book and make contact with those you love. So check your e-mail and get networking because Respected Master T'ung reminds us that everything is open to us and, that being the case, all we have to do is to take part. Clearly this is a day when exciting new avenues can be explored if we make an effort, and there is no better way than to make contact with others, so remember that the Chinese say:

 When two persons are of one mind, their sharpness can cut through metal.

Monday December 13 – The Earth Pig – Essence of the day is Wood

At this time of year, the yin energy is very strong and until the Winter solstice it is getting stronger every day. Not surprising then that the portents are again very difficult and this can only result in confusion and misconception. It is important to remember that this is the Water time of the year and looking inward for solutions and answers is preferable to looking to others to provide direction. Rest and recuperation are ideal ways to spend days like today, especially during the Winter season when the aim is to conserve energy rather than find ways to expend it.

Tuesday December 14 – The Metal Rat – Essence of the day is Earth

Try to avoid outside activities today such as building, construction, agriculture or anything that requires heavy manual labour. Trading and business dealings are well favoured, although the T'ung Shu Almanac warns against the use of savings. A good day to catch up with correspondence and deal with paperwork in general, so if you are falling behind in that department it might be wise to attend to it today. Travel may be a little tricky, so perhaps it would be wise to consider doing those things nearer to home, rather than dashing around all over the country.

Wednesday December 15 – The Metal Ox – Essence of the day is Earth

A day of cleansing, and since things have not been going too well recently, perhaps it would be wise to clear out any rubbish that may have accumulated either in the home or at work. It is surprising how much we acquire on a week-to-week basis and this requires regular maintenance in order to prevent it from building up. Traditional Chinese homes treat this very seriously and the T'ung Shu Almanac has a complete section called 'Mr Chu Tzu's Guide to Managing Your Home'. This is full of advice on how to live a good life and be a good neighbour and there are wonderful little illustrations depicting various activities. One of them shows someone sweeping outside the house with the Sun coming up in the background. The caption advises us to rise at daybreak and sweep away all the dust and to remember to keep the inside and outside of the home clean at all times. This is really fundamental for good feng shui, so if things feel as if they are piling up, clear them out and sweep them away.

Thursday December 16 – The Water Tiger – Essence of the day is Metal

Marriage ceremonies are very auspicious because it is said that all who marry today will receive great honours within the community. Moving home is also favourable today, so if you had planned to move into your new home in time for Christmas, today is a very good day to do it. Travel is also indicated as a suitable activity, particularly if you are planning to travel a long distance, and anyone leaving on holiday today is particularly fortunate. Not only do the influences denote that the holiday will get off to a flying start, but also that Heaven is clearly in favour of your choice of departure date. Whatever you do, try to avoid menial tasks and choose something more challenging – after all, the portents are favourable and when things are going well there is no better time to try to utilise opportunities at your disposal.

Friday December 17 – The Water Rabbit – Essence of the day is Metal

If the events of yesterday are still continuing, then today is equally favourable, so everyone should try to use this beneficial energy to enhance their lives. For those of you who have finished, now is a good time to reflect on future plans and to consider what changes could be made to enable you to improve your lives in the coming year. Remember, Winter is a time for reflection and looking inward, and a time to collect your thoughts and your energy in preparation for a new beginning in the Spring. This also applies to ideas and it is always good at this point in the year to look at what you want to achieve next year and how best to implement your ideas to reach your objectives, whatever they are. Planning is a crucial aspect of any campaign, so if you are at a loss today and find yourself with spare time on your hands, spend at least some of it considering your aspirations.

Saturday December 18 – The Wood Dragon – Essence of the day is Fire

Mixed fortunes today, but a day which favours activity, with the exception of travelling by boat because the T'ung Shu warns of shipwrecks. Apart from that, you can take your pick: inside, outside, business or pleasure, it doesn't really matter, because, with the exception of laziness, anything goes. One thing we are warned to avoid, however, is making accusations of any kind. Although this should always be remembered, it is particularly appropriate today, because we are warned that there will be dire consequences for those who ignore this advice. So bear in mind the words of the ancient Chinese sage who said:

 Do not attack people behind their backs because it will only rebound on your family.

Sunday December 19 – The Wood Snake – Essence of the day is Fire

All the emphasis today is on the home and any activity involving the home is considered to be auspicious, with the exception of moving into a new one, which we are advised against. Domestic activity is very favourable and it would be good to get any DIY jobs out of the way, but, above all, we should remember, 'If your home is happy then things run smoothly'. Once the boring, mundane tasks are out of the way you can consider other more pleasurable aspects of domesticity like having a dinner party or a family get-together, because the portents favour this approach today; so if you feel you need an excuse for a party, you have one – it's called going with the flow.

Monday December 20 – The Fire Horse – Essence of the day is Water

This is the day of the Fire Horse and he has chosen a difficult time to make his last appearance for this year. A day of conflict, quarrels and confrontations, and everyone would be well advised to stay clear of any situations that have this potential. There is nothing to gain at times like this, apart from new enemies and they are not beneficial for anyone, so keep this in mind and exercise restraint if you are confronted with a difficult situation. Equilibrium is always the key – even though it may sound too simple to be true – so if you are faced with aggressive, passionate energy, a calm and passive response is the only hope of balancing the situation. It is all a question of maintaining the essential balance of yin and yang.

Tuesday December 21 – The Fire Sheep – Essence of the day is Water

An improvement on yesterday but still not a day to force issues of any kind. The Chinese say, 'Beat the grass to startle the snake' but today you would be well advised to leave even the grass alone because if the snake wants to come out, it will and you will have to cope with it – and if it doesn't, forget it. Not a day to go running up a mountain with the wind against you, so go with the flow; it's a case of what works, works well, but what doesn't work, simply will not – and it is not a reflection of your efforts, it's just the way it is today. Make life easy for yourself and tackle only those tasks that don't present any problems. That way you will not only get through the day unscathed, but you will also achieve something.

Wednesday December 22 – The Earth Monkey – Essence of the day is Earth

Today is not only the Full Moon but also the solar festival of Tung Chih, which is the mid-point of Winter and marks the Winter solstice, still regarded in China as a major festival. At one time this was considered to be the New Year and it is the time of year when the yin energy is at its peak. After today, the new yang energy begins to grow and from now on the days begin to get longer as the nights get shorter. We often forget this but it is a comforting thought, especially if there is snow around and the nights are especially cold. Today, many traditional Chinese families will gather together and enjoy a huge feast that the entire family attends. It is a day of giving thanks for our families, for our food and for the new yang energy that will influence our lives over the coming year. It is interesting to note that the last time the Winter solstice took place on a day of the Full Moon was back in 1961, which was, in retrospect, a watershed marking the beginning of a prosperous decade. That is a good sign for the coming millennium, which hopefully will prove to be another favourable milestone in human history.

Thursday December 23 – The Earth Rooster – Essence of the day is Earth

A good day for trading and for drawing on savings, which many will no doubt do as they complete their Christmas shopping, so an excellent time to go to town to visit the shops and look for gifts for friends, families and loved ones. This Christmas, in particular, there will be a real air of expectation as we are constantly reminded of the forthcoming millennium, and this will result in everyone being more hyped up than usual, even for this time of the year. No doubt this will be reflected in the fact that everyone will be running around today as if the end of the world is nigh. It isn't, of course, but there is no doubting the power of millennium fever.

Friday December 24 – The Metal Dog – Essence of the day is Metal

Today is the birthday of Amitabha, meaning 'boundless light', the Buddha who taught that nirvana could be attained through faith as well as through meditation. He is a very popular figure and his birthday is a time for sincerity and repentance, which are very appropriate virtues for Christmas Eve. An excellent day to get in touch with friends and family, again very appropriate for this time of year, and no doubt there will be many people chatting away on the telephone, over the Internet and over a few drinks at their local bar. Try to keep in mind the deeper aspects of Christmas and light a few candles not only for baby Jesus, but also for Amitabha and for all the prophets and sages who through the ages have tried to encourage everyone, in their own way, to live in harmony and at peace with the world. It is important at this time of the year to remember that behaviour is more important than ceremony.

    There are 300 rules of ceremony and 3,000 rules of behaviour.

Saturday December 25 – The Metal Pig – Essence of the day is Metal

Merry Christmas everyone! No doubt the children will be up early as usual but if you are listening, let mum and dad get a little more sleep! I am sure you will all be happy with your presents but you don't have to say 'Thank you' straight away, especially if it's still dark. A day that suits family events, although everyone should take care not to upset other family members, so be careful not to overindulge. This should be a day of joy and celebration and if everyone makes the effort, it will be. In this sometimes overly materialistic world, children often get caught up in the latest craze and this can put pressure on parents, especially those who are less fortunate. Don't be too hard on children who don't seem to be as appreciative as you feel they ought to be. They will learn by watching your appreciation.

Sunday December 26 – The Water Rat – Essence of the day is Wood

An energetic, active day that will suit all kinds of activities, so even if you are unfortunate enough to be working today, don't worry, because it will still be a good day and if you maintain a positive attitude and an enthusiastic approach, you can benefit from the favourable influences just as well. The T'ung Shu Almanac advises against long-distance travel, heavy manual labour and also breaking into savings, so it's not a good day to go to the sales unless you have put aside some spare money for the occasion. If this is the case, then you are certain to find a few bargains but beware of slick marketing, because today favours the shopkeeper.

Monday December 27 – The Water Ox – Essence of the day is Wood

Jogging, swimming and sport in general are very favourable today and there is an emphasis on matters relating to health. With New Year's Eve looming and more parties and socialising on the agenda, perhaps it would be wise to have a rest today to allow the body to recuperate. No doubt the house could do with a clean-up and it would be wise to get rid of any rubbish that has accumulated, which at this time of year is quite considerable. A day of preparation then, because the next item on the agenda is New Year's Eve 1999, which will arguably be the biggest celebration of the last ... how many years? If it's all too much already, take yourself down to the local health spa and treat yourself to a session of your favourite therapy to help you switch off from the chaos.

 The answer to noise is silence.

Tuesday December 28 – The Wood Tiger – Essence of the day is Water

An auspicious day and one which favours activity and big events – the bigger the better. If you are getting married today, congratulations – not only for your wedding but also for selecting such an auspicious day. The Almanac informs us that Heaven bestows its bounty on new unions solemnised today, which will result in a happy and prosperous life. Heaven's treasuries are filled to the brim, we are told, so clearly a very auspicious day and one that everyone should try to utilise to the best of their ability. Don't waste time on petty, mundane tasks but leave those for another time, because there are much more important matters to attend to.

Wednesday December 29 – The Wood Rabbit – Essence of the day is Water

If you are still partying, then you may as well carry on for today at least, because this is really just an extension of yesterday. Having said that, it is also a good time to look around, see what is going on and decide if there is anything that you can do to improve the situation. With a new year approaching on such an historic occasion as the passing of another millennium, this really is a good time to reflect on what you would like to achieve next year and how you are going to accomplish your aims. Even if you are stuck in a rut, this period will pass, you will move on, and when you look back you will wonder what the fuss was all about. We all have the power to change our lives. It may take some time but the quicker we start, the sooner we will accomplish it, so don't delay any more. Think positive and look to the future and remember:

 Every action begins with a single thought.

Thursday December 30 – The Fire Dragon – Essence of the day is Earth

Today is the birthday of Chang Kuo, one of the eight Heavenly Immortals, who is often depicted riding a white mule. Legend has it that the mule was able to travel thousands of miles a day and when Chang Kuo reached his destination, he was able to fold the mule up like a piece of paper and put it in his wallet. When he wanted to travel again, he took out the sheet of paper, splashed water on it and it turned back into a mule. A novel alternative to a foldaway bicycle and far superior! He is also known as 'the giver of sons' and his image is often seen above the bed of newly weds. A day of mixed fortunes but one that will benefit those who keep themselves busy, even if they do so by having too much fun to worry about anything else.

Friday December 31 – The Fire Snake – Essence of the day is Earth

Today must be the party night of the century for many people, who have no doubt been planning this for quite a while now. Yes, it's New Year's Eve 1999 and it represents the biggest party in living memory, so it is good that all the portents are fairly favourable today. Relaxing and entertaining are very compatible, but we are advised against too much movement, so perhaps that it is warning not to burn ourselves out tonight – after all, we have another thousand years to look forward to. This won't prevent everyone from going out and going absolutely mad because it's the end of 1999, but you should be prepared for an anti-climax and if you wake up tomorrow morning wondering what it was all about, you shouldn't be surprised.

Saturday January 1 – The Earth Horse – Essence of the day is Fire

Many people will no doubt still be at the party, or sleeping off the effects, but there are sure to be more hangovers than usual today and as a result, some may not be in the best of moods. The T'ung Shu Almanac warns against conflict today, so if you do have a headache, be careful not to use that as an excuse to be argumentative, especially with friends and loved ones. Conflict is a terrible thing and something that we should constantly strive to avoid, and this can only be achieved through cultivating our minds. Clearly, only when we are balanced can we really perceive the full impact of reality, and anger renders that impossible. Chinese philosophy teaches us:

 When one is angry, the mind loses its balance and then things are watched but not seen, listened to but not heard, and eaten but not tasted.

Sunday January 2 – The Earth Sheep – Essence of the day is Fire

For those who have been celebrating since Friday, today provides the perfect opportunity for a well-deserved and much-needed rest. Certainly a day to go with the flow, because the portents are not favourable towards anyone who wants to force things today. Hopefully, everyone will be so tired out after all the recent celebrations that the last thing on anyone's mind will be to impose their will on others. With celebrations so huge this year, the hangovers will probably be even more numerous and worse than usual, so leave others to sleep it off and if you are feeling the same way, then follow suit, because you will all feel better tomorrow.

Monday January 3 – The Metal Monkey – Essence of the day is Wood

An auspicious start to the week and a favourable day for all kinds of activities, especially long-distance travel; so if you have planned a winter holiday and you are leaving today, you have chosen well. This is a day when opportunities will present themselves, so it would be wise to keep this in mind and stay alert, because you never know what might turn up. There is a lovely story of two men sitting under a coconut tree. One man looks up at the coconuts and knows that they will eventually fall down, so he sits there waiting patiently. The other man looks up and realises that he can climb the tree and pick the fruit now and so up he goes. Don't be like the man who sits and waits. Today the fruit is there for the taking, so even if you feel a bit depleted, you should make the effort to get up that tree for if you don't, others will get there ahead of you and there will be nothing left to fall down for you.

31

Tuesday January 4 – The Metal Rooster – Essence of the day is Wood

Mixed blessings today, but a good day for trading and business in general and, since it is also considered to be favourable for using savings, perhaps there are some bargains to be had at the sales. Of course, this should not be used as an excuse to be reckless but, if you apply yourself to what you really need, then you will no doubt pick up a few bargains. For those at work, today provides the opportunity to get back into the swing of things and since we are nearly in the last month of Winter, it is a time when we should begin to consider the coming Spring and how we can apply ourselves over the coming year in order to move forward in a positive direction.

 Heed the end no less than the beginning and your work will not be spoiled.

Wednesday January 5 – The Water Dog – Essence of the day is Water

A day of recuperation – at least that is what the T'ung Shu Almanac suggests – and an excellent day for the arts, so anyone involved in music, painting or any of the performing arts should feel extremely inspired today. Anyone attending a concert or exhibition is sure to be even more moved than usual because the performers will probably excel themselves. The reason for this is that the arts are associated with the element of Water, the essence today is also Water and we are in the season of Water. All this enhances the favourable portents, resulting in additional support from the natural energy cycles, so why not harmonise with this energy and consider visiting the theatre or going to a concert or art gallery?

Thursday January 6 – The Water Pig – Essence of the day is Water

Today is the solar festival of Hsiao Han, which means 'little cold', and it marks the beginning of the month of the Ox, the last month of Winter. As the name suggests, this is the time of year when it really begins to get cold. Snow is water in its frozen state and this can create obstacles because it cannot drain away or flow freely. This is one of the reasons why Water is also associated with danger as well as communication. The Water element is again enhanced by the essence of the day and this may result in many people becoming more emotional than usual. We should all try to avoid looking too deeply into things because the chances are we will only arrive at the wrong conclusion. This is the last day of this lunar month and as always, there is no Moon and this will only encourage negative thoughts, so wait until the New Moon and see how different everything looks.

Month 12

As always with a new lunar month, it begins on the day of the New Moon, the last for this year, according to the Chinese calendar. Not an auspicious start to the month because all the portents are fairly gloomy, so today is not a good day to get married, open up a new business or begin a new venture. The T'ung Shu informs us that this is the day of concealment, so perhaps we should all remain as quiet as possible today. This is perhaps appropriate after all the recent activity when even the strongest among us are likely to be feeling a little tired. A day of rest and recuperation then, appropriate for the Winter season when we should all be trying to conserve our energy.

Saturday January 8 – The Wood Ox – Essence of the day is Metal

Today has a much more active feel about it and it is a good day for trading and business in general, so if you have matters to attend to, don't delay, do them today. You may be tempted to go shopping, because the Almanac suggests this, but we are warned against the use of savings, so bear this in mind. If you are prone to overspending, give it a miss today, because fortune favours the shopkeeper and as a result you may well end up buying a lot more than you intended. The wise approach would be to concentrate on things that need attention rather than things that may or may not need purchasing, because that way the day will be far more profitable. It is always good to get your priorities right, as we are reminded by the Chinese proverb that says:

 The old priest sold his temple but kept his gods.

Sunday January 9 – The Fire Tiger – Essence of the day is Fire

A good day for cleaning, clearing and sweeping away, so today would be a sensible day to tidy up after the New Year celebrations if you haven't already done this. As we enter another new year, it is good to clear out negative thoughts, ideas and feelings that represented obstacles in the past. Feng shui remedies are very favourable today and they can play an important role in achieving this. If you are single and hoping to attract a new partner, the worst thing you can do is to sleep in a single bed because this denotes that you have no room for anyone else in your life. If this applies to you, then treat yourself to a new double bed, throw away all the old sheets that you may have shared with your previous partner, get rid of all those old photographs of ex-lovers and get yourself a new life.

Monday January 10 – The Fire Rabbit – Essence of the day is Fire

Anyone attending an important function today is very fortunate and there is every indication that it will be particularly successful. This applies to matters relating to business and pleasure, so, whether you are attending a wedding or an important business meeting, put on your best smile and enjoy it. Today represents an excellent opportunity to get the week off to a flying start and with such favourable influences, everybody would be wise to try to tap into them, because many things can be accomplished. Not a day for the faint-hearted but one that will favour the brave and those motivated enough to make good use of it.

Tuesday January 11 – The Earth Dragon – Essence of the day is Wood

A much quieter day today, except for those still carrying on the business of yesterday, who can proceed with confidence. For the rest, a day to sit back and consolidate their position rather than trying to catch up. Outdoor activities are not favourable, so if you want to tackle some jobs around the home, think inside and not outside. Balance is the key, as Respected Master T'ung reminds us, and if you are not the star of the show, keep out of the limelight and let those who are, shine. If you don't wish to attract attention, then keep in mind the Chinese proverb that says:

    A familiar sight attracts no attention.

Wednesday January 12 – The Earth Snake – Essence of the day is Wood

Today should be full of activity because the portents are very favourable, so everyone should try to tap into this wonderful, exhilarating energy. Not a day to sit back and observe, but a day to take part and achieve. Sometimes we prevent ourselves from moving forward, often because of past experiences – hence the expression 'Once bitten, twice shy'. The Chinese have a different way of looking at this and they say: 'Every time this man sees a rope, he thinks it's a snake'. While this may prevent us from getting bitten too much, this attitude often prevents us from making use of opportunities that come our way, so have a good look at that rope – the chances are that it is not a snake after all.

Thursday January 13 – The Metal Horse – Essence of the day is Earth

If you had planned to move into a new house today, then perhaps you should reconsider and select another day because the T'ung Shu advises against it. It is important to get the best possible start when you move into a new home and, as the Chinese would say, 'Why take the chance?'. Travel is also frowned upon, so a day to stay local unless you cannot avoid it, and if you must travel and you are driving a long way, be particularly careful. If you are travelling by public transport, the chances are there will be delays, so allow plenty of time. If you are stuck at home today, you should try to make use of your time in a productive way, because domestic matters are considered to be very suitable. After the chores are out of the way, you are free to enjoy the fresh air and that's not a bad deal, so cheer up, even if the weather is gloomy.

Friday January 14 – The Metal Sheep – Essence of the day is Earth

It is imperative that everyone avoids conflicts of any kind today, because the T'ung Shu warns that these will only result in serious consequences. There is an irritable, conflicting feel about today that will encourage confrontation and the best course of action would be to try to keep out of the way. Even with the best of intentions, it is not always easy to avoid aggressive behaviour in others, but quite often it is the result of a combination of factors rather than one specific incident and can even represent a cry for help. Empathy and understanding are the best responses because they offer the only way to bring some balance into the situation. It would seem appropriate that we remember the words of Lao Tzu, the founder of Taoism, who said:

 The female overcomes the male with stillness.

Saturday January 15 – The Water Monkey – Essence of the day is Metal

Today is the festival of Ju-Lai Fo and this day commemorates the Buddha Sakyamuni's enlightenment. Prayers are offered today for help and guidance, especially by the hierarchy who traditionally made sacrifices on this day. Light candles, burn incense and ask for inspiration, because it is there for the asking, but remember: if you don't ask, you won't get. We are in the last part of the Water period for the year, because in a few days we will enter the Winter Earth season and this will provide everyone with an opportunity to adjust themselves and to prepare for the coming Spring.

Sunday January 16 – The Water Rooster – Essence of the day is Metal

An auspicious day today that favours activity of all kinds, including travel – good news for those who have a lot of dashing around to do, because clearly the portents are in their favour. The emphasis is on energy and this applies to business as well as pleasure, so the only thing to avoid is doing nothing. Respected Master T'ung reminds us against making malicious comments about other people, so be careful not to damage other people's reputations and avoid any form of gossip. We don't like people talking about us and therefore we should not talk about others. The Chinese proverb says:

> *What you do not like from those above you,*
> *do not do to those below.*

Monday January 17 – The Wood Dog – Essence of the day is Fire

A good day for business and trading in general when no doubt many will be busier than they expected, so stay alert and be on the look-out for any opportunity that may come your way. Today is the first day of the Earth season, Winter Earth, and a time to make ourselves ready for the coming new season, which in this case is the Spring. This is the time to prepare the ground to enable the seeds that we plant in the Spring to have a better chance to grow and flourish. It is important to remember that any work put in now will pay dividends in the Spring – it is very much a question of the more we put in, the more we can expect to get out.

Tuesday January 18 – The Wood Pig – Essence of the day is Fire

An auspicious day in many respects and coupled with favourable portents; someone somewhere is bound to strike it rich. The finding of hidden treasure is predicted today in the T'ung Shu, so everyone should keep their eyes open, especially those attending sales or auctions of any kind – even if it is a jumble sale – because although not everyone will discover a missing Picasso, the indications are that someone might and it could be you! One thing is certain: opportunities will present themselves today and it is up to us to try to capitalise on them as best we can.

Wednesday January 19 – The Fire Rat – Essence of the day is Water

Mixed fortunes today. It is a day that suits paperwork rather than manual labour, so if there is any correspondence that needs chasing up, today is a good day for it. Calm and quiet should be the order of the day and although this may not suit everyone, you would be well advised to listen because failure to heed this advice may result in regret. Expectations should be kept to a minimum because Respected Master T'ung points out that although there may be goods on display, all the shops are closed for business. This means that you would be better spending your time contemplating your prospects for the coming year, rather than setting off in search of them.

 A great wind does not blow all morning; a heavy rain does not continue all day.

Thursday January 20 – The Fire Ox – Essence of the day is Water

Another day that favours business and commerce, but we are advised to avoid long journeys and heavy manual work. Although trading could be very lucrative today, it would be wise not to use any savings, because the Almanac suggests that we keep our treasuries closed today. A very good day to start a new venture and for beginning new projects and since this also applies to relationships, there may be a few who meet their soulmate today. Of course, this can only be achieved by taking part in the activities, so go with the flow and instead of looking for excuses to say 'No', think of how many different ways you can say 'Yes'.

Friday January 21 – The Earth Tiger – Essence of the day is Earth

Today is the solar festival of Ta Han which means 'great cold', and as the name suggests, this is often the coldest part of the year. It is the mid-point of the last month of Winter, which means that we are not far away from Spring – a pleasing thought when the weather is inhospitable and depressing. At this time of year, it is good to remind ourselves that Spring will soon be here, so nurture your vitality, balance your mind and begin to think of all the things you wish to achieve this year because it all starts in Spring. It is appropriate that one of the portents today reminds us to pay attention to our health, not only our physical well-being but also our spiritual energy and emotional needs.

37

Saturday January 22 – The Earth Rabbit – Essence of the day is Earth

Mixed blessings, but still a very active day suitable for all kinds of big events and functions, so not a day to waste on petty issues. Travel is well favoured and it is also considered to be a good day to move into a new home, so if that is on your agenda, you have chosen well. The secret is to spend time on important issues, no matter what they are, so whether you need to spend time with your partner to discuss delicate issues or whether you need to speak to your boss about a pay rise, today is the day. Not a day for hesitation but a day to reach for the stars and hope for the best; even if things are not going well, bear in mind the Chinese proverb that tells us:

 It is on bad fortune that good fortune leans.

Sunday January 23 – The Metal Dragon – Essence of the day is Metal

A day to relax and rejuvenate the mind, body and spirit and a good day to focus on future events. This is a stabilising period and it should be used to balance ourselves so that when Spring arrives we are prepared for the new, invigorating energy. At this time of year, with the prospect of Spring just around the corner, it is good to reflect on our hopes, dreams and aspirations for the future and to see in what ways we can adjust and alter our efforts in order to bring these to fruition. Much can be accomplished in the Spring and even more so when we are prepared for it, and there is no better time to begin our preparations than now.

Monday January 24 – The Metal Snake – Essence of the day is Metal

This week begins on a favourable note today and encourages activity of all kinds: the worst thing that you can do is to do nothing. So seize the day and go for it; today is a day when things can be achieved. There are no excuses, we can do the job. For those at work, today presents an ideal opportunity to begin the week on a positive note and, if this is utilised, it provides us with a chance to benefit from these favourable influences surrounding us.

Tuesday January 25 – The Water Horse – Essence of the day is Wood

Another auspicious day that will favour everyone, although we should all try to avoid moving home or travelling too far today. Domestic activity is very favourable because the emphasis from all the portents is on the house. It is important for the home to be a peaceful haven as we all perform better when our home base is secure, but there is also another reason. In *The Art of War*, by Sun Tzu, we are reminded that without harmony at home we are only inviting trouble. This is very true because when things are going well at home, it can be the source of an enormous feel-good factor and something from which we can derive a sense of strength. We should remember this today in particular and keep in the mind the words of Sun Tzu, who said:

 An enemy with troubles at home is ripe for conquest.

Wednesday January 26 – The Water Sheep – Essence of the day is Wood

There are plenty of benefits available if you can avoid conflict today, although that might be quite difficult because there is sure to be a lot of it about. There is a lovely Chinese fable about a clam who was sunbathing and minding his own business when a large bird swooped down on him. The clam shut his shell very quickly and trapped the beak of the bird, resulting in a stalemate. Neither would let go of the other and after a while a fisherman came along and caught them both. We should learn that if we are engaged in conflict, it can be very difficult to find a way out, and more often than not there are only losers in the end.

Thursday January 27– The Wood Monkey – Essence of the day is Water

Not exactly an auspicious day today, and we have no choice but to do the best we can with it. One thing is clear: we must avoid applying force to anything, because today not even gentle persuasion will be effective. The Chinese believe that you cannot explain something to someone who doesn't want to understand and if others don't want to take your opinions on board, there is nothing you can do about it. Go with the flow and make life easy for yourself today, because there is nothing to be gained from trying to please others; and in that case, you are far better off pleasing yourself.

Friday January 28 – The Wood Rooster – Essence of the day is Water

A big improvement on yesterday; today everyone can utilise the favourable portents for all types of activities. A good day to get married, because we are told that children born of a marriage today will fill their pockets with gold and precious gems. It is also a good day for socialising, because another indication is harmony, with men and women spending their time enjoying themselves – clearly a good day for a party. In many traditional Chinese homes, incense is burnt and candles are lit at midnight and the kitchen god is taken down and smeared with honey before the image is burnt. This symbolises sweetening him up so that he will make a good report to Heaven and the family will then be favoured by the gods.

Saturday January 29 – The Fire Dog – Essence of the day is Earth

Another excellent day to make use of the many opportunities that should be available, provided of course that you are alert and remain open to beneficial changes. Today is suitable for many things including, trading, studying, building and construction, so take your pick. Provided you do something, you are certain to benefit. Today is the day when the kitchen god presents his report to Heaven regarding the behaviour of the family over the past year, but if you have behaved yourself and conducted yourself properly, you have nothing to worry about – and in any case, you can always turn over a new leaf now.

Sunday January 30 – The Fire Pig – Essence of the day is Earth

The arts are well favoured today, so anyone attending a performance of any kind, will not be disappointed. A good day for reading, studying, painting, playing a musical instrument and anything else that doesn't involve heavy manual work. It is also a day of rest and recuperation, which is very appropriate for a Sunday, so perhaps it would be wise to go with the flow, chill out and relax. In this the last period of Winter, it would be a good idea to take advantage of opportunities like today to nurture and store vital resources and to build up our reserves in readiness for the coming Spring. There is plenty of activity to come, so there is no point in burning yourself out before it has even started. Relax and enjoy the peace and quiet and remember:

 Learning consists of adding to one's stock day by day.

Monday January 31 – The Earth Rat – Essence of the day is Fire

Not the most auspicious start to the week that we have had, but there have to be some downsides. On the one hand we have a favourable indication of seizing opportunities, but on the other hand we are informed that everything is shut, so it's a case of having a ticket but missing the bus. The best thing to do is to expect nothing today, but at the same time still make an effort to make any improvements you can, without making life difficult for yourself. If you are at work, it would pay to slip gently into your usual routine and, if you can do this, at least you will be in harmony with the influences of the day, even if you don't achieve everything that you would have liked to. Don't panic – the week has only just started and things will improve.

Tuesday February 1 – The Earth Ox – Essence of the day is Fire

A good day to go to a sale or an auction because the portents favour trading, bargaining and business in general. Outside activities are not considered to be auspicious and travel is also not very favourable, so it would be wise to avoid these if possible. A day to look out for any opportunities that may appear, especially those that relate to business, although new ventures of any kind are also favourable, including relationships. If yesterday was a bit sluggish, then today will see a definite improvement and that should encourage everyone who has things to do, places to go and people to see.

Wednesday February 2 – The Metal Tiger – Essence of the day is Wood

The T'ung Shu Almanac informs us that today is the day of cleansing and since Spring is nearly here, it would be wise to use this opportunity to clear the decks in preparation for the new rejuvenating energy. It is always nice to start with a clean sheet and it would be very good to give the house a good clean, so that when the new kitchen god is placed on the wall, his first impression is a good one. Health matters are also indicated today, so, if you have been meaning to make an appointment to see the doctor or the dentist, don't put it off any more. Feng shui remedies are clearly very favourable and, with the Chinese New Year just around the corner, it would be very good to start clearing away clutter, rubbish and debris from the old year in order to make space for the new, invigorating energy.

Thursday February 3 – The Metal Rabbit – Essence of the day is Wood

Traditionally, this is the day when the North Star visits Earth to make a judgement on the events of the year. This is a day of forgiveness, and in traditional Chinese homes the whole family gather and forgive each other for their mistakes, failings and wrongdoings over the past year. It is the time to wipe the slate clean, to forgive and forget and to encourage a new start when the New Year arrives. This is a lovely sentiment and one which we should all aspire to, because we all make mistakes, and without forgiveness there is no hope for any of us.

Friday February 4 – The Water Dragon – Essence of the day is Water

This is the Chinese New Year's Eve and this year it coincides with the solar festival of Li Chun which marks the beginning of Spring. Since it is the last day of the year, it is associated with the day when all the Buddhas come down to Earth to judge the evil actions that have taken place over the year. We all have an opportunity for a fresh start tomorrow and it would be very wise today to reflect on our actions over the past year and to identify how we can improve our lives, our relationships and our environment, and how we can live in harmony with others – not just our friends, family and loved ones, but with everyone, even ourselves.

Month 1

Today is the first day of the Chinese New Year and as always it begins with a New Moon. If you are still exhausted after the millennium celebrations and are looking for something to provide you with an additional boost, remind yourself that Spring is here and with it a New Moon, a New Year and a fresh opportunity to revitalise your life. This is often the day when many traditional homes using popular feng shui remedies place a new ba gua, or pa kua, mirror outside the home, above the main door, to deflect any negative influences that may approach the house. During the course of the year, they become depleted and a little the worse for wear, so it is considered to be very good feng shui to replace them each year. As well as a time for celebration, today is also a day when the family shrines are decorated, candles are lit and offerings are made to all the occupants of Heaven. In traditional Chinese homes, a new image of Lao Chun, the kitchen god, is placed on the wall today to remind everyone, including the children, that he is not only watching over us but that he will also present his 'report' to Heaven at the end of the year. In feng shui terms, the kitchen is the heart of the home and his presence is a reminder that Heaven is constantly observing our thoughts as well as our actions.

This is considered to be the birthday of Chung-li, one of the eight Heavenly Immortals, who is also known as Chung-li Ch'uan. A former soldier who rose through the ranks to be the marshall of the Empire, he was reputed to have gone into retreat as a hermit. One story says that while he was meditating, he discovered a jade casket hidden in the wall, that contained the secret of immortality. He is also regarded as the distributor of wealth, since another legend states that during the time of a great famine, he was able to turn copper and iron into gold and silver, which he distributed to the poor. The T'ung Shu Almanac advises us that today is very auspicious for all kinds of activities, so make use of the fresh Spring energy to blow away the cobwebs and start to rejuvenate your life.

Another auspicious day which favours domestic activities in general but, if you don't feel like doing the housework, why not invite a few friends and have a dinner party instead? The emphasis is on the home, so whether you are feasting or going through the household accounts, you will be going with the flow. Gardening is also considered to be very favourable today and since one of the portents in the Almanac relates to the opening of wells, if you have decided to build a water feature in your garden to help improve the feng shui, today would be a very good day to start work. A well-tended garden with plants and shrubs always helps to improve the environment and any contribution is sure to be rewarded. That is why the Chinese say:

He who plants a garden plants happiness.

Tuesday February 8 – The Fire Monkey – Essence of the day is Fire

The T'ung Shu Almanac warns us that there is a lot of conflict in the air today and that it would be wise to stay clear of arguments of any kind. This applies especially to those in authority, so if you get caught speeding or you find yourself in trouble over where you have parked, however rude the officer or warden is, resist the temptation to tell them what you really think. Prevention is always the best measure, but if you do get caught up in any conflict, try not to make things worse, because they may escalate out of control.

Wednesday February 9 – The Fire Rooster – Essence of the day is Fire

Today is a vast improvement on yesterday and the emphasis appears to be on business affairs, which we are told will prosper and flourish. Weddings are also well favoured and it is said that those who marry today will receive 'official recognition', so even if it is only a humble affair, the Emperor will surely hear of it. The only thing that we are warned against is going against the flow, symbolised by one of the portents that describe ascending a perilous mountain. So if things are going well, carry on, but if they are not quite working out as you had planned, walk away and look at them again tomorrow from a different perspective. In the words of the ancient Chinese sage:

A wise man without fortune waits for good fortune.

Thursday February 10 – The Earth Dog – Essence of the day is Wood

A very auspicious day to get married: not only are we told that all who marry on this day will be very fortunate, but travel is also considered to be favourable, so clearly the honeymoon will get off to a flying start. With the fresh, new Spring energy, now is the perfect time to begin new undertakings and to plant the seeds for future hopes and dreams. Buying land and starting construction is also particularly favourable today but any activity will prosper. The only bad things to do is nothing at all or, even worse, to pursue malicious gossip which will return to haunt us if we ignore this advice.

Friday February 11 – The Earth Pig – Essence of the day is Wood

Not a particularly fortunate day in some respects, but a good day for trading, and although the Almanac suggests that it is also a good time to make use of savings, these should not be used for anything too speculative, especially if it involves land or property. Contemplation and meditation are also very well favoured today and the energy is particularly conducive to study and education. The Chinese place a very high value on the study of books, especially those that relate to personal cultivation.

The pursuit of other things is small,
the study of books excels them all.

Saturday February 12 – The Metal Rat – Essence of the day is Earth

A day of mixed blessings really, so make the most of the beneficial aspects: it would be a good day to attend to any letters that need writing or to make any telephone calls that you have been meaning to do. An excellent day to get networking, so get your address book out, check your e-mail and start contacting people. Spring is a time for laying foundations and planting seeds but you still have to get out there and do it, because although the natural energy cycles are working with you, they cannot change your life without your support. It pays to remember the Chinese proverb that says:

A star, however willing, cannot help the Moon.

Sunday February 13 – The Metal Ox – Essence of the day is Earth

Today is the birthday of the Jade Emperor, who is considered to be the chairman of the board when it comes to Heaven. It is said that everyone has to report to him, including the other two Pure Ones, Tao Chun and Lao Tzu. Jade is often associated with purity and the Jade Emperor is thus considered to be the purest of all the gods, even on a par with Sheng Ti, the one true god. If you are attending a funeral today, take heart, because even though it can be a very distressing time, the Almanac reminds us that any family who attends a funeral today will be assisted by those who have recently passed on. Prior to the arrival of Buddhism, traditional Chinese thought did not include a concept of Heaven and Hell and regarded reincarnation as something natural. Just as death was seen to follow life, life was seen to follow death in accordance with the principles of yin and yang.

Monday February 14 – The Water Tiger – Essence of the day is Metal

It is appropriate that today is Valentine's Day because the Constellation of the day is known as Hsin, which is associated with the heart. This was often connected with the Emperor, because people are considered to be the heart of Heaven and Earth and the Emperor is considered the master of people. Today is also the festival of the Earth god and anyone with a garden, however small, should consider making a little earth shrine to protect the home and the garden. Many traditional Chinese homes have one and they are also found in every village, often outside important buildings. Today these shrines are decorated, candles are lit and offerings are made to the Earth god, who represents Heaven's authority here on Earth. It would be very good feng shui to light a few candles in the garden tonight with your Valentine as a token of your love for each other and it feels very appropriate to end with a Chinese proverb that says:

 If you desire happiness, you must first cultivate the heart.

Tuesday February 15 – The Water Rabbit – Essence of the day is Metal

A very good day to carry out feng shui remedies in the home or at work, especially those designed to sweep away negative influences. Space-clearing would be very favourable, but this does not only apply to our living space: this is also a good time to clear away negative thoughts and ideas in order to make room for the fresh inspiration that Spring always provides. Health matters are also highlighted today and as a result sport, fitness and health regimes are all very well favoured, along with any visit that you may need to make to your doctor, dentist or therapist. Spring is a very active time for plants, animals and people and it is very important at this time to pay attention to our physical well-being, much in the same way that we would put our car in for a service before setting out on a long journey.

Wednesday February 16 – The Wood Dragon – Essence of the day is Fire

A very good day for important meetings, conferences and weddings so, combined with the active Spring energy, today is not the day to sit around feeling sorry for yourself, but a day when great things can be achieved. One of the portents indicates that any new opening instigated today will double one's fortune, and if that is not enough motivation, we are also informed that the whole family will prosper as a result of these efforts. Clearly, then, a day to go for and make use of it, whatever it is, because now is the time to act.

 Those who can talk are not equal to those who can perform.

Thursday February 17 – The Wood Snake – Essence of the day is Fire

The portents are a little confusing today. On the one hand we are told that the Constellation indicates general good fortune, but on the other hand we are advised to sit back and contemplate future plans rather than tackling outstanding tasks. What is important is to remember that our intentions should always be pure, because one of the creatures associated with today is said to be able to distinguish right from wrong. With that in mind, it is wise to remember the words of Confucius, who said:

> *Wealth and position are desired by everyone,
> but one would rather not have them if to attain them
> requires the use of unscrupulous means.*

Friday February 18 – The Fire Horse – Essence of the day is Water

Today would be a very good day to make a special effort for your partner, to take the time to let them know how much you appreciate them. One of the portents today is associated with the Ox Boy, who is forever separated from his lover, the Weaving Maiden, whom he is only allowed to meet for one day each year. Today is unfortunately not the day and this serves as a reminder not to take our partners for granted. If you want to strengthen your relationship with your partner, it is important to remember this and consider how you would feel if you were in the same position as this unfortunate couple. The fact that you see your partner every day should not make them any less special.

Saturday February 19 – The Fire Sheep – Essence of the day is Water

Today marks the solar chi festival of Yu Shui, which can be translated as 'rain water' and this denotes the coming of the Spring rains, essential for young plants. This is the mid-point of the month of the Tiger, associated with the first month of Spring, so ideas, hopes and aspirations all need nourishment, just as young plants do. Since the essence of the day is also Water, the energy of the day is definitely going to favour those who begin to propagate ideas and plans that will enhance their life at a later date. This is also the day of the Lantern Festival, which traditionally marked the end of the New Year celebrations and as a result presents the last opportunity to celebrate the New Year. It would be very appropriate to have a candlelit dinner this evening, with candles in the kitchen, candles in the bedroom, in fact, candles everywhere. For an authentic lantern festival, visit your local Chinese store, which will no doubt have a selection of paper lanterns. This evening, weather permitting, wrap up in plenty of warm clothes and have a barbecue. Soak up the fresh Spring energy and contemplate how to make the most of the coming year.

Sunday February 20 – The Earth Monkey – Essence of the day is Earth

It is important to avoid disputes today, especially domestic ones. This cannot be emphasised too much because the portents in the T'ung Shu are all in agreement. Quarrelling, arguing and gossiping will only result in grief and unhappiness, which will not benefit anyone. It is surprising what a few kind words or gestures can accomplish and this is often the best way to respond to negativity, because it offers a balance. When the opposite approach is taken, things escalate out of control, creating even greater obstacles. Certain days are appropriate for discussions and negotiations but today is not one of them.

Monday February 21 – The Earth Rooster – Essence of the day is Earth

Not a particularly favourable day for travelling, according to the T'ung Shu Almanac, especially by boat, and although both the portents relate to warnings of danger, if we keep this in mind, there should be no cause for concern. One of the Chinese characters for the day resembles the roof of a house and this may denote accidents in the home, so bear this in mind. Monday mornings are not the easiest of times as we are forced to focus on the coming week and returning to work, but a positive attitude does help enormously. Try to consider the benefits that always follow achievement of any kind and remind yourself that even if it is a cold, wet and generally dreary Monday morning, it is still Spring. Achieving something on a day when the odds are against it can be a wonderful source of motivation, because it reminds us of what we can achieve when everything is in our favour or, as the Chinese would say:

      The measure of your success is determined by
how well you can perform during the bad times.

Tuesday February 22 – The Metal Dog – Essence of the day is Metal

Everyone should make use of the very favourable energy today which encourages activity of all kinds. Building work that is started today is particularly favoured, because the Chinese character for the Constellation represents a house with wealth. This applies not only to buildings but also to any businesses and new ventures that are initiated today. With the support of the Spring energy, this is the perfect day to do something that you have always wanted to do, but have never managed. The essence of the day is Metal and this will help to support anyone who may be lacking in will-power, but only if they make an effort. If further motivation is needed, the T'ung Shu informs us that the Emperor will grant favours to those who follow this advice and that their families will become wealthy and live in harmony. Clearly any effort made today will not go unrewarded.

Wednesday February 23 – The Metal Pig – Essence of the day is Metal

Another important day on the feng shui calendar, because it is the day of celebration in honour of the door gods. Colourful paper posters would have been pasted to the wall on either side of the front door at the New Year, and today incense is burnt and candles are lit as a tribute to the work these warrior guardians will carry out in watching over the home and business. Many people have already adopted another approach by placing two tigers by the main door. They are often known as temple dogs because of the custom of placing them outside temples to discourage negative energy from entering.

Thursday February 24 – The Water Rat – Essence of the day is Wood

Although we are told that the Emperor of Heaven's messenger is out of danger today, not everything is perfect. Business matters are very well favoured and whether you are chasing up unpaid accounts, trying to secure new business or creating new openings, your efforts will be enhanced and as a result your chances of success improved. Communication of any kind is also very favourable today and this includes music, painting and the arts, so whether you are performing, practising, exhibiting or merely attending, you are certain to receive an additional burst of inspiration. Try to avoid working in the garden and if you are considering a feng shui water feature outside the home or business, resist the temptation to begin work today, because the Almanac does not consider disturbing the earth to be very auspicious.

Friday February 25 – The Water Ox – Essence of the day is Wood

Very much a day of mixed blessings but the emphasis is definitely on the family. At the end of the week, it is always good to unwind with family and friends and tonight would be a good time to spend at home with those we love and cherish. In this modern, hectic and often chaotic world, we frequently neglect the simple things in life, like staying home and playing games with the children or spending time alone with our partner, exchanging thoughts and ideas. Tonight is very conducive to doing all of the above and if you had planned a visit to your local restaurant, bar or cinema, why not consider having a family night in, as an alternative? The Almanac suggests that if this advice is heeded, peace and harmony will flourish within the home, allowing a much healthier and happier flow of energy like the Chinese ballad:

The family gather like an orchestra, each member playing his part, and together they help to create beautiful music reflecting their common purpose, harmony within the heart.

Saturday February 26 – The Wood Tiger – Essence of the day is Water

An auspicious day in many respects, but only if you keep active. The Almanac informs us that if we keep busy and make use of the Spring energy, much can be accomplished. All manner of business activities are favourable, so whether you are selling or buying, you are certain to be encouraged. With this in mind, if you have been overspending recently and you feel like going shopping, perhaps it would be wise to leave the plastic at home, because today, the shopkeeper will also do very well. This is also emphasised in the T'ung Shu where we are advised against the 'opening of the storehouse'. The most sensible course of action today would be to use this active energy to catch up on any work that you have put to one side, and to prepare for the week ahead.

Sunday February 27 – The Wood Rabbit – Essence of the day is Water

It would be wise for everyone to unwind and relax because this will be the most effective remedy for what is a fairly unfavourable day that does not really encourage positive activity. A good day for Spring cleaning, clearing out the attic or the spare room and, of course, for implementing feng shui remedies in the home, especially those connected with the family and relationships. Alternatively, if this has been done or it doesn't sound very appealing, treat yourself to a day at the health spa. Yoga, aerobics, t'ai chi or even jogging in the park would all be very much 'in the flow'. Even as a spectator, you are playing your part, so if the last thing you feel you need is physical exercise, then take the kids to see a football game or some other spectator sport and that way you can still absorb the fresh Spring energy.

Monday February 28 – The Fire Dragon – Essence of the day is Earth

There is no time for Monday morning blues, because today will present all kinds of opportunities for those who are prepared to make an effort. The Constellation today is Pi, which signifies a net, often used to trap and capture game, indicating the ability to seize opportunities. Weddings, meetings, conferences and important occasions are all very favourable and, with the additional benefit of the active Spring energy, it is clear that much can be accomplished today. Not a time to dwell on unimportant, mundane issues; instead, put all that behind you and adopt a positive approach to everything you do and towards everyone you meet. There is much to be gained from today, but only by participating can we expect to reap the rewards on offer, because we should all remember the Chinese proverb that says:

Heaven is not sparing of its doctrine,
nor Earth of its treasure.

Tuesday February 29 – The Fire Snake – Essence of the day is Earth

For those in the flow, today should present no difficulties because it represents a natural extension and conclusion to yesterday. However, if for one reason or another you failed to get started, then just take some time out to reflect how you can get back on track. Sometimes we lack the confidence to 'go for it', often brought on by the feeling that we lack the tools to do the job. Financial, emotional and physical problems all help to create a negative attitude towards our hopes, our dreams and our aspirations; and it is very easy to put ourselves down. Only by taking a positive, optimistic attitude towards life can we really hope to improve our situation.

 An insect can only fly ten paces, but if it can attach itself to a noble horse, it can travel a thousand miles.

Wednesday March 1 – The Earth Horse – Essence of the day is Fire

Another day which favours activity of all kinds, especially anything to do with building, construction, agriculture and landscaping. Definitely a day that favours outside activities and anything to do with the Earth, so, if you are fortunate enough to have a garden and you have been neglecting it recently, today would be a good time to make a start. Feng shui is about harmony and any clutter, rubbish and untidy areas only serve to diminish the positive energies. The Almanac illustrates this point in a section called 'Chu Tzu's Guide to Managing Your Home', which provides a benchmark for family behaviour. One of the things highlighted in this section is the need to sweep the outside of our house every morning as an indication that we treat the outside of the house with the same respect that we give to the interior.

Thursday March 2 – The Earth Sheep – Essence of the day is Fire

If you are attending an interview for a new job, sitting an examination or attending an important lecture, then you can afford to relax a bit, because fate has been very kind and the beneficial influences encourage these pursuits in particular. Outside activities are also very well favoured, so it is another good day to get out into the garden. We are advised against travelling and the T'ung Shu also warns against moving into a new house today, so if you had planned to do that, consider selecting another day. The Chinese would never think of moving into a new home on a day that the Almanac said was inauspicious, even though they are renowned as a nation that loves gambling.

 If they gamble continuously, even gods and fairies lose.

Friday March 3 – The Metal Monkey – Essence of the day is Wood.

Today is Geng Shen day, which refers to the Stem and the Branch of the day, and this is regarded by many as the time when the natural energy cycle begins a new phase. You would do well to keep this in mind today, because it may encourage you to spend some time on your own. The portents suggest a day of conflict and if you are attending a difficult meeting or you find yourself having to act as a mediator, then try to remember not to face the east and confront the Grand Duke. Better still, try to position yourself so that you are facing west and as a result you will receive his support. With so much conflict indicated, anyone faced with a difficult situation will need all the help they can get.

Saturday March 4 – The Metal Rooster – Essence of the day is Wood

Going with the flow will again pay dividends today. It is very much a case of ignoring, for once at any rate, the advice that says 'If at first you don't succeed, try again': today if it doesn't work, leave it. If things are going well, you have nothing to worry about, but don't exhaust your energy trying to force anything – whether it's an idea, an opinion or even a piece of machinery. If anything unexpected does come your way, then take a good look at it because the Almanac informs us that new openings discovered today could be gateways to disaster. It further informs us that if we are unable to achieve anything of any worth today, then we should drink wine and be happy, which is very appropriate for a Saturday night but, as always, keep things in moderation – or should I say, in balance.

Sunday March 5 – The Water Dog – Essence of the day is Water

Today marks the solar chi festival of Ching Chih, which can be translated as 'excited insects'. This next solar fortnight, or solar chi, is one of the most active, indicating a time when insects come out of hibernation. This applies to everything – plants, animals, ideas and plans – so it is the perfect opportunity to move up a gear and start trying to make things happen. At this time of year everything becomes more active, as the yang energy coupled with the activity of Spring enables the beginning of growth and the process of regeneration. It is a New Moon again tomorrow, so try to tune into the emerging fresh, invigorating energy and consider how you can make the best use of it. If you have feng shui crystals in your home, it would be very good feng shui to clean them today, to enable them to absorb more of the forthcoming fresh energy, thus making them even more effective.

Month 2

Monday March 6 – The Water Pig – Essence of the day is Water

As always with a new lunar month, it begins on a day of the New Moon, which always brings new positive energy. This certainly applies today because all the portents have very positive connotations, which should encourage everyone in whatever they do. Weddings, functions and travel are particularly auspicous. There are always exceptions, of course, and we are warned against saying anything that may harm others. With such favourable conditions, it would not be wise to try to prevent others from enjoying the same beneficial energy, so try to be generous towards everyone today.

Tuesday March 7 – The Wood Rat – Essence of the day is Metal

Although today is not quite as favourable as yesterday, it is very appropriate that it is the birthday of Mencius because many of the portents indicate success for those involved in education in any way. Students, teachers and professors can all benefit today as the energy is very much geared towards study, contemplation and education. Mencius was a highly regarded Confucian scholar and philosopher who, like the great Irish master, Oscar Wilde, was able to deliver the most profound statements with ease. The brilliance is only matched by the simplicity of the statement, merely reflecting the principles of yin and yang. A good example of this is a quote from Mencius which we should all keep in mind:

> Those who follow that part of themselves which is great are great men, but those who follow that part which is small are small men.

Wednesday March 8 – The Wood Ox – Essence of the day is Metal

Another very auspicious day today, which again has an academic flavour since it is the birthday of Wen-ch'ang, the god of literature. For those looking for inspiration, motivation or encouragement in their pursuit of literary success, try lighting a candle in honour of Wen-ch'ang and ask him to support your endeavours. Business matters can also benefit today, which should encourage us all to make an effort to use this stimulating energy to inspire and motivate others. If you are planning to get married today, you have chosen well because the Almanac implies that the children born of a marriage today will become very talented and as a result they will bring honour to their parents.

Thursday March 9 – The Fire Tiger – Essence of the day is Fire

The Almanac informs us that the portents are in conflict today, so it is very much a case of the yin with the yang. On the one hand the indication is of new beginnings and growth, and on the other we are informed that everything is closed for business. This very much reflects the scenario of having a ticket for a bus that does not exist, rather than missing it altogether – it's a bit like being all dressed up with nowhere to go. If you feel like this today, try not to let it put you off your stride, because although you may feel that you are taking one step forward and two steps back, this is not really the case, it's just nature playing one of her little tricks.

Friday March 10 – The Fire Rabbit – Essence of the day is Fire

Matters relating to the home are considered to be very important to the Chinese and this is reflected in the various sections that are printed in the T'ung Shu every year. To the Chinese, there is an art to running the home in such a way that peace and harmony prevails. Money is obviously very important and generating wealth is something that every family is concerned about. It is not surprising then that we are reminded from time to time to look at our own accounts, and today we are advised to pay any outstanding bills that we have put to one side. According to the principles of yin and yang, only by paying others can we expect to be paid ourselves, and by paying our own bills, we encourage others to pay theirs.

Saturday March 11 – The Earth Dragon – Essence of the day is Wood

Feng shui remedies would be very suitable today, especially those connected with improving relationships with our elders in particular. The Almanac reminds us that we should all respect the elderly people in the community, not only those who are family members, and this should be kept in mind. If you really want to go with the flow today, try to offer help or assistance to an elderly person, then consider yourself very fortunate because nature has seen fit to employ your services. If that is the case and you go about your task with a cheerful and enthusiastic disposition, you never know what job she may give you next time. Remember:

Opportunities given by Heaven are far greater than the advantages offered by Earth.

Sunday March 12 – The Earth Snake – Essence of the day is Wood

Everyone should try to make use of the very favourable conditions today, which encourage all the things relating to Spring, such as growth, new beginnings and rejuvenation. Weddings, meetings, seminars and gatherings of all kinds are sure to benefit from the active Spring energy that is now gaining momentum. If you are moving into a new house today, you have chosen very wisely – the T'ung Shu is very specific about this. One of the portents is the Chinese character Fang, which can relate to the house or the room, and it is considered to be a very good day to build. This can also apply to acquiring a new house, and with other portents informing us that today is a good day to change one's residence, anyone moving into a new home today has certainly made a fortunate choice.

Monday March 13 – The Metal Horse – Essence of the day is Earth

Not exactly the ideal start for another week, although it could be a lot worse and, if you are prepared for a slow start to the day, then at least you will not be disappointed. Try taking a positive approach by spending a little time looking at the week ahead, what you want to achieve and how you can best go about it. If you are already in a routine or you are in the process of concluding what was started yesterday, than you can proceed with confidence, because the elements are in still in your favour.

Tuesday March 14 – The Metal Sheep – Essence of the day is Earth

There are no excuses today: everything denotes active, stimulating and encouraging influences that everyone can tap into. The key word is 'activity', so the worst thing that you could do would be to stay in bed and feel sorry for yourself. It may be cold, it may be wet, it may even feel miserable, but that changes nothing, because at the end of the day it is still Spring. The Almanac does not usually encourage speculation, but every now and again the influences are so favourable there is almost nothing that cannot be achieved and today is a good example. Even treasure hunters are in harmony today because we are also informed that someone, somewhere, is certain to locate 'hidden treasure'. Clearly, opportunities are abundant.

 He who acts with energy has a strong will.

Wednesday March 15 – The Water Monkey – Essence of the day is Metal

A very favourable day when we should all try to realise our hopes and dreams. If you are at work, look around for inspiration to enable you to expand your ideas. If you are at home, try to find ways to create more space, to allow room for expansion within the home to take place. Families, businesses, plants, animals and even ideas, hopes and dreams all need room to grow, and it is important at this time of the year, when growth is so rapid, for all these things to have sufficient space. This is very much what feng shui is all about – recognising that everything should have its place and that only by creating a space for everything can we keep things in balance.

Thursday March 16 – The Water Rooster – Essence of the day is Metal

If you can avoid negativity, you can continue to enjoy the support of the natural energy cycles but if not, today may present obstacles that may disrupt your flow. We all tend to resent authority at times, but if you have reason to deal with anyone in authority today, you would be well advised to take a softly, softly approach. Authority is not always in control, but today is one of those days where the criminals not only get caught, they get punished as well. Crime is one of the more undesirable aspects of society and its causes and effects are very complex, although it can basically be seen as another example of the yin with the yang. In a modern world that revolves around success and accomplishment, there has to be a balance, because:

 If people in one place are prospering, people in another place are suffering.

Friday March 17 – The Wood Dog – Essence of the day is Fire

It is perhaps fortunate that it is the end of the week. It is often frustrating when things don't work out the way we would like and sometimes this is difficult to accept. Often, in our determination to carry something through, we are inclined to push a little too hard and this usually results in a negative reaction. It is good to encourage change and growth but this must also be allowed to happen naturally and today we are reminded of that fact. The T'ung Shu also has a sense of humour, for we are told that if we are having difficulties we should give up, walk away and drink wine. It is good to unwind when we feel agitated and if you have had a difficult day, then enjoy a drink with a few friends and try to see the funny side of life, because tomorrow is another day.

Saturday March 18 – The Wood Pig – Essence of the day is Fire

Long-distance travel is very auspicious today, so if you are leaving home for a while, take heart, at least you are going with the flow. If the reason is due to business, it may well herald the beginning of something new and exciting that will serve to enhance your life at a later date. If you are taking a holiday, then there is every chance that it will be the start of a new period that may prove to be a turning point. Keep busy, don't sit around moping, there is always something that you can be getting on with. Ignoring this advice may, according to the Chinese proverb, leave you feeling:

 Like the kettle in the tea shop, always boiling.

Sunday March 19 – The Fire Rat – Essence of the day is Water

The Constellation today is referred to as Hsu, which can be expressed as the void and is particularly associated with family quarrels. Do keep this in mind today if the family are spending time together because it may explain a lot. It is a reflection of irritation, like an itch that always arrives before a wound gets better. The yang energy is about to take over and after a Winter of hibernation, it is raring to go and sometimes it is not properly directed. The best advice would be to get out in the fresh air if things get a little heated at home. Don't worry too much about anything that is said in the heat of the moment; all families have their disagreements, after all, as the Chinese say:

 No family can hang up the sign, 'No trouble here'.

Monday March 20 – The Fire Ox – Essence of the day is Water

Today is the solar chi festival of Ch'un Fen, which marks the Spring equinox, the point at which yin and yang energy is finely balanced and day is equal to night; but from tomorrow yang takes over as the days get longer. This is one of nature's natural markers, reminding us that this is a time of growth, expansion and invigorating chi, and we should all learn to make use of it. You may wish to make a list of all the things that you would like to have completed by the Summer solstice in June and try to make use of all the available active energy in order to achieve this. Today is also the birthday of Lau Tzu, or Lao Chun, who is thought of as the founder of Taoism. Possibly his greatest work is the *Tao Teh King,* a study of life, in which we are reminded of the circle of life:

 The crooked becomes straight, the empty becomes full and the worn-out becomes new.

Tuesday March 21 – The Earth Tiger – Essence of the day is Earth

Another day of mixed blessings, but, with the emphasis still on the active yang energy, it would be wise to continue to explore and nurture new ideas and plans. The Almanac advises us that it would be wise to spend at least part of the day attending to correspondence, so if you have been meaning to contact someone, don't delay any more. Business always flourishes with the addition of new contacts and today is the perfect time to chase up leads, or just spend time looking at what the Internet has to offer. Advertising is also well favoured today, so why not look at other ways that you can promote yourself and your services? Don't be like the Chinese proverb that says:

 When a mirror is hung with the glass against the wall, there is no reflection.

Wednesday March 22 – The Earth Rabbit – Essence of the day is Earth

An auspicious day which reflects ample opportunities for anyone who is looking to begin a new venture or who is looking to expand in a new direction. Business activities of all kind are considered to be very favourable, so if you are out shopping, take it easy, because today most definitely favours the shopkeeper. Anyone who is attending an auction or a sale should benefit but it is important not to overextend yourself financially, because the Almanac warns against the use of savings. Outside activities are also not considered to be 'in the flow', so perhaps today would not be a good time to start digging the garden.

Thursday March 23 – The Metal Dragon – Essence of the day is Metal

Another ideal day for carrying out feng shui remedies around the home, especially if these are being carried out to clear away unwanted, stagnant energy. Clutter not only causes obstacles that prevent the chi from circulating around the house but also takes up valuable space that could be used to encourage new things to come into our lives. The break-up of a relationship can be a very painful experience and we are often reluctant to let go of old photos and letters from previous partners. From a feng shui point of view, this can often prevent us from meeting new people, because we have not created a space for them to enter our lives and by keeping old photos and letters we are symbolically refusing to let them go. In Chinese thought, it could be argued that you will be unable to meet a new partner because you are still clinging on to the old one.

Friday March 24 – The Metal Snake – Essence of the day is Metal

An active day which will suit big occasions, especially weddings, because it is said that children born of a marriage today will always have their pockets full of silver. When the portents are auspicious and they encourage growth and expansion, there is no better time to make use of the invigorating Spring energy, so bear this in mind today. Job interviews, important meetings and events of all kinds should all benefit today, and whether you are meeting Bill Gates or the Queen of England, you can proceed with confidence and if you can position yourself to face the west and have the Grand Duke supporting you, who knows what you might achieve. Today is also the birthday of Kuan Yin, the goddess of mercy, who is the most popular of all the deities in China. She is the embodiment of the female principle and she is associated with compassion, love and forgiveness, which she dispenses liberally without judgement. Light a candle in her honour today and bear in mind the following:

 Riches adorn a house, but virtue adorns a person.

Saturday March 25 – The Water Horse – Essence of the day is Wood

Another very good day to utilise the prevailing energies, so if you are busy at work or in the home and you are continuing with the activities of yesterday, then nothing should really disrupt you. When things are going well, we should try to make the most of it because as we all know things do not stay the same. The Chinese place an emphasis on exploiting one's own good fortune and, when things are going well, making that extra little effort can often turn a good result into a great one. It won't always be Spring, so the best advice is to try to utilise its full potential while it is here, and that way you will increase your chances of success in the Summer.

Sunday March 26 – The Water Sheep – Essence of the day is Wood

A difficult day in some respects: the Almanac warns us that we should all be very careful what we say to others, because today is associated with legal action. We are also told that unless they are absolutely necessary, they will result in unhappiness and misery for those involved. The secret is not only to keep busy, but also to stay out of the way of others who are unaware of the underlying influences today. The good news is that we are also told that the Emperor of Heaven has arranged everyone in their places, so providing you go about your business quietly, there is no reason why you should encounter any difficulty. The secret is not to provoke anyone or let anyone provoke you, because you may regret it if you do.

Monday March 27 – The Wood Monkey – Essence of the day is Water

An excellent start to the week which could prove to be very productive for many, since not only are we informed that opportunities abound today, but that we also have the means to make good use of them. Good news for those involved in business who may be trying to conclude a deal today, or for those looking around for a bargain. If you are stuck at home, don't feel that you are missing out, because wherever you are is where the action is, so keep your eyes open as there will be something that you feel like doing. Try to avoid too much travel and if you had planned to move into a new house today, consider another day for it, because although it is very favourable to buy one today, it is not considered auspicious to move in.

Tuesday March 28 – The Wood Rooster – Essence of the day is Water

The flow is interrupted today but only temporarily, so don't allow any negativity to affect you too much. We should expect a bad day now and again and if we adopt a healthy attitude to the yin and yang of life, it need not alter or change our course. There are always negative influences around, but today it is very important to be aware of this and to avoid them. Respected Master T'ung advises us that today is associated with P'o, which relates to ruin brought about by conflict and quarrels, and he is so concerned that he suggests that we all pack up and go fishing – obviously to keep out of harm's way. Of course, this is not always practical but you could always pin a note to the door saying 'Gone fishing' – after all, who is to know any different? This is a day where there is very little to gain but much to lose, so keep in mind the Chinese proverb that says:

> As the light of a single star can light many regions,
> so a single unguarded action can ruin the virtue
> of many good actions.

Wednesday March 29 – The Fire Dog – Essence of the day is Earth

A vast improvement on yesterday and if you are apprehensive about going back, you can relax; because yesterday has now passed and things will begin to balance out a bit. Difficulties may still exist but unless you are foolish enough to take an arrogant attitude towards them, they will become resolved in time. Allow the conflicting energy to pass and focus on the things that you can have a positive impact on and direct your energy towards those. Very much a day to go with the flow and not take things too seriously. Enjoy what you do, try to take a light-hearted view and do not expect too much for your efforts.

Thursday March 30 – The Fire Pig – Essence of the day is Earth

Harmony returns, which is very appropriate, because today is considered to be the birthday of the ruler of Heaven and it is a time to celebrate all the occupants that dwell in the palace above. It would be a very nice gesture – not to mention good feng shui – to acknowledge this today by lighting candles in honour of the occasion and by telling others the good news. Heaven is also regarded as the source of helpful people and the best way to attract helpful people into your life is by being a helpful person. Knowledge is a wonderful thing, which the Chinese prize very highly, but study must never be carried out as a form of self-indulgence. After all, as the Chinese proverb says:

 The purpose of learning is to enable us to teach others.

Friday March 31 – The Earth Rat – Essence of the day is Fire

A peculiar end to the week, because the Constellation today is Kuei, which refers to the Ghostly Carriage, and this may account for any strange happenings that may occur. This may well have a beneficial effect for some, especially those who are engaged in meditation or occupied with their studies. A good day for trading of all kinds and the Almanac even suggests the prudent use of savings, but don't let that be an excuse for reckless expenditure – there will be other opportunities. If you are considering a little speculation, try to be realistic and don't allow your expectations to become unreasonable; in this way, you will improve your chances of success.

Saturday April 1 – The Earth Ox – Essence of the day is Fire

Another day of mixed fortunes when emotions may be running high, and for some it may well end in tears. The Constellation is Liu, associated with the weeping willow, suggesting that nothing can take place that will not turn out badly. Fortunately, this is balanced out by the fact that other portents are very favourable, which means that today can still be very prosperous, but it is a question of attitude. If you are experiencing a fortunate phase and things are going well, it can be argued that you have a responsibility towards those who are less fortunate, and the more success you enjoy, the greater that responsibility. Everyone needs a little help from time to time and by offering help and assistance we encourage positive aspects not only in others but also within ourselves, and this enables us all to grow.

Sunday April 2 – The Metal Tiger – Essence of the day is Wood

This is known as the day of concealment or containment, and it can have very positive effects for those who wish to use today to stop smoking or begin a new diet or any other new regime that is designed to improve their lives. If you are spending the day at home and you want to make a positive contribution, you may like to consider spending some time catching up on any mail that you have put to one side. If you are inclined to a more energetic approach, then clear out the garage or the spare bedroom. Energy stagnates if it is not kept moving and there is nothing better to rejuvenate the house than fresh, positive Spring energy. Listen to the Chinese proverb which says:

 If you wish to attract the south wind, open up the north window.

Monday April 3 – The Metal Rabbit – Essence of the day is Wood

An auspicious and encouraging start to the week which particularly favours new ventures because this is the day of Chien, to 'establish'. Although it is not printed in red – indicating that it is especially lucky – this does not diminish the positive aspects for one moment. Today is also linked with the Constellation Chang, which can be likened to a net which is spread out, denoting that you have everything covered, so increasing the chances of success. The fact that we are in Spring is the most important factor to take into consideration: there is no better time to begin a new venture or to establish a new position.

Tuesday April 4 – The Water Dragon – Essence of the day is Water

Today marks another important solar chi festival, Ch'ing Ming, which can be translated as 'clear and bright'. This heralds a change in the weather as Spring begins to really flourish and all signs of Winter begin to disappear. It is a very important festival in China and it is a time when families visit the graves of their ancestors in order to tidy them up and to make offerings on their behalf. To the Chinese, everything can be viewed as symbolic and this approach is used by many today, who burn paper money, printed by the 'Bank of Hell', to credit the accounts of their ancestors. This money can then be used to bribe the corrupt officials who naturally reside there, thus making a better 'life' for themselves. It would be very good from a feng shui point of view to acknowledge this today and even if you are unable to visit a family grave, you could polish the picture frames of family members who have passed away, put some fresh flowers near them and spend a few moments in quiet thought.

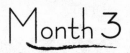

Month 3

Wednesday April 5 – The Water Snake – Essence of the day is Water

As always with a new lunar month, we begin on a day of the New Moon, which always brings a new, fresh burst of energy, especially during the Spring. Many traditional Buddhists fast on the day of the New Moon to cleanse the body and allow a bigger 'space' within which to store the fresh, new, vibrant energy. The advice in the T'ung Shu Almanac echoes these sentiments and suggests that we look at our homes, as well as ourselves, in the same way. Feng shui is therefore very appropriate today and anything that is carried out to improve the flow within the home or to make space for revitalising energy will be very beneficial. We are also advised to attend to our health, so if you have been meaning to make an appointment to see a doctor, then don't delay any further – do it today.

Thursday April 6 – The Wood Horse – Essence of the day is Metal

Another very auspicious day which encourages matters of importance, whether they relate to business or pleasure. The Constellation of the day relates to Ch'io, which is associated with the Dragon of the east and therefore Spring. Ch'io is regarded as the 'horn' of the Dragon and it is considered to be a very good day to get married or buy land for a new house, and for new ventures in general. We are in the last few weeks of the Wood period after which we enter the Earth Season, which will provide us all with the opportunity to take a little breather before Summer begins. Even if you feel exhausted after the energetic Spring, it is important to keep the flow going a little longer.

Friday April 7 – The Wood Sheep – Essence of the day is Metal

For those who are in full flow, today should provide an opportunity for a very successful conclusion to the events of yesterday. Conferences, meetings and conventions can all end on a flourishing note today, inspiring confidence and enthusiasm, vital ingredients that encourage growth and expansion of ideas, projects and relationships. If you have concluded the business of the week, then it would be wise to sit back a little and reflect on the future, contemplating ideas that can enhance your life, your home and your own sense of well-being. The Almanac informs us that it would be futile to chase up new opportunities today because they are not yet within reach, so bear in the mind the Chinese proverb that says:

 Only a silly dog chases the flying bird.

Saturday April 8 – The Fire Monkey – Essence of the day is Fire

A good day to keep busy and to try to keep your mind on the job in hand and not let others distract you. The Almanac suggests that all the indications are that today will be wet and windy, which describes the energy perfectly, so bear this in mind and be prepared for a bit of a battle against the elements. For those who are determined to make an effort at all costs, outside activities are very favourable, so you could consider spending the day working in the garden. The Summer is not so far away and any work put in now will certainly pay dividends when the sun is shining and we want to make use of this valuable space. A tidy garden is not only pleasing to the eye but it is also good feng shui, as the Almanac constantly reminds us.

Sunday April 9 – The Fire Rooster – Essence of the day is Fire

An auspicious day in many respects and one that favours things connected with the home, although we are also warned that it would not be a good day to move into a new house. Domestic activity is considered to be very favourable, and since travel is not regarded as particularly fortunate it would seem to be a good day to spend at home. The family benefits from spending time together and although we are all aware of this, it is often overlooked in our modern, hectic and competitive world. It is good to try to encourage the family to work together as a team and if there are jobs to be done around the house today, it is surprising how quickly they can be achieved if everyone makes a contribution.

Monday April 10 – The Earth Dog – Essence of the day is Wood

An inauspicious day, to say the least, and one that brings with it a lot of negative influences, but there is a bright spot on which to focus and one that helps to balance things out. It is always good to try to make use of positive influences, while at the same time being aware of the less favourable ones. The most favourable aspect of today is the fact that it is the birthday of Ch'ang Lao, a venerable old monk who was blessed because of his philanthropic acts. He is often associated with the elderly and any help and assistance that we can offer to the more senior members of our society will be looked upon with particular gratitude by Ch'ang Lao today. For many, this is a day of celebration for the elderly, and celebrating and acknowledging this fact will be far better than getting involved with the today's negative aspects, which denote conflict with serious consequences.

Tuesday April 11 – The Earth Pig – Essence of the day is Wood

A vast improvement on yesterday, although not a day when everything can flow as we would like, and, as a result, many may find the energy a little frustrating. Going with the flow is always the best option, but especially so today, so it is important to relax and let events dictate to you rather than you trying to control them. This may not always be convenient since our lives and careers are often based on schedules and timetables, but we should not forget that nature has her own agenda, which may differ from ours. Going with the flow is all about avoiding friction, which is achieved not by imposing our will but by following nature's natural cycles. As the Chinese say:

 Ride a horse to catch a horse.

Wednesday April 12 – The Metal Rat – Essence of the day is Earth

There is no time to lose, because today is very favourable for all manner of things. The Spring energy is still here and is very much boosted by the fact that the Constellation relates to the tail of the Spring Dragon and Respected Master T'ung informs us that it is the day of Ch'eng, which means completion. This denotes that today presents a golden opportunity to make use of this favourable, active energy to initiate new beginnings of any kind. Additional motivation, if any were needed, is the fact that the Almanac also informs us that those who follow this advice today will prosper greatly. The bad news is that it also represents the last real opportunity to do this for this year. We will be entering the Earth Season soon and after that move into Summer. However, in order to make use of the Summer, we have to do our work in the Spring, as the Chinese classics often remind us:

 Do the things pertaining to Spring during the Spring and not during the Summer.

Thursday April 13 – The Metal Ox – Essence of the day is Earth

Another day when much can be achieved and everyone should try to make use of this last burst of Spring energy in its vibrant Wood state. Remember, this is a time of growth and expansion and this relates to everything – plants, animals, hopes and fears – so the emphasis should be directed towards the more beneficial aspects, especially regarding negative situations. It is a very good day for trading and business in general and the T'ung Shu even approves of the use of savings. As long as you can spot a good deal from a bad one, you can afford to take a more speculative approach to business today.

FENG SHUI ALMANAC 2000

Friday April 14 – The Water Tiger – Essence of the day is Metal

Today should provide favourable conditions for a successful end to the week and it would be wise to try to conclude as much business as possible. A day to finish the job, if you are at work, so keep this in mind and encourage yourself to complete as many tasks as possible. You will be helped by the fact that you will be going with the flow but that does not take away the responsibility that you have to initiate proceedings. Music, painting and the arts in general are all favoured and the Almanac also indicates that some of those who have been suffering with an illness recently will begin to recover today.

Saturday April 15 – The Water Rabbit – Essence of the day is Metal

Another day when you can use the unfavourable energy to your advantage by selecting today as a time to put a new regime into action. An excellent time to give up smoking, stop biting your nails or to instigate a new health programme or anything else that requires determination and will power. The T'ung Shu also advises us that it is an appropriate time to renew contact with old friends and colleagues and, considering that it is still Spring, following this advice could well lead to new and possibly exciting avenues. If you still need convincing, then consider the Chinese proverb that says:

 When one branch shakes, a thousand leaves move.

Sunday April 16 – The Wood Dragon – Essence of the day is Fire

Today is the last day of the Spring Wood, because tomorrow the Earth Season begins and the influences today reflect this fact. It is very appropriate that today is Sunday, a time when most people get at least some time off, and it is important for us all to remember this today. We often take for granted the work carried out in the home by our partners who stay at home to look after the children, but they need some time off as well. Try to ensure that they too get a bit of time to themselves today. Children can also play their part today, especially the older ones, who can all help to give mum a break. After all, as the Chinese say:

 The ideal mother-in-law is still not as good as
one's own mother.

Monday April 17 – The Wood Snake – Essence of the day is Fire

The Almanac suggests that we try to avoid travel today, by either land or sea and presumably by air as well. Definitely a day to stay grounded and, since this is the first day of the Earth Season, why not bear this in mind and take a little time out to check your position? This is a period of balance and a time to take a compass bearing to ensure that we are on course and on target. Once Summer arrives, we will be in full swing again and before we launch into this next phase, nature has seen fit to provide us not only with some respite, but also with some balancing, grounding energy to allow us to make any adjustments necessary to improve our flow.

Tuesday April 18 – The Fire Horse – Essence of the day is Water

The elements today favour those who don't wish to waste their time on menial tasks because the emphasis is on matters of importance. This applies to everyone, not only to those in business so, whether you are getting married, negotiating the biggest deal of your career or moving into your new home, make the most of it. The same can be said for those who need to make an important decision, which should not be viewed as a dilemma but as an opportunity to enhance the quality of life. Every time we are faced with a decision, an opportunity presents itself, even if we are unable to see it, because in every yin there is a yang, although sometimes we have to look for it.

Wednesday April 19 – The Fire Sheep – Essence of the day is Water

Today is the day of the Full Moon and emotions may be running a little high, so please bear in mind that Respected Master T'ung reminds us that it is the day of P'ing, which can be translated to mean 'adjust' or 'harmonise'. Balance is the key and harmony is the name of the game, so rather than expect others to adjust to our requirements, perhaps it would be appropriate for us to do the changing today, not just with others, but also within ourselves. At this time of the year, during the first of the four Earth seasons, we have an opportunity to balance ourselves and to make any alterations necessary before embarking on our Summer voyage and all the excitement and action that the Summer Fire brings. Summer is a time when things flourish and prosper, but this also applies to the negative aspects of life and it is important to try to clear as many of these as possible away before the Summer arrives, to prevent them from thriving as well. We have the power, we only have to exercise it and if we do, we will prosper because, as the Chinese say:

He who depends upon himself will attain the greatest happiness.

Thursday April 20 – The Earth Monkey – Essence of the day is Earth

Today marks the solar chi festival of Ku Yu, which translates as 'corn rains', which are essential for a good harvest. This represents the last solar fortnight of Spring and the emphasis is on nourishment and a time when we begin to 'feed' our ideas, hopes and aspirations in order to help them flourish and prosper over the coming Summer. It is also the birthday of Ch'un Ti, the goddess of light, who the Taoists refer to as the queen of Heaven. She is also known as Tou Mu, goddess of the North Star, and like Kuan Yin, she is worshipped and adored by Buddhists and Taoists alike and also Hindus, who refer to her as Maritchi. She is depicted as having at least eight arms and she is usually seen holding the Sun and the Moon. Images, statues and figurines of her are quite common and anyone who has one of these in their house or at work should light a candle in her honour today and spend a few moments in quiet contemplation as a mark of respect for the good work she carries out.

Friday April 21 – The Earth Rooster – Essence of the day is Earth

A favourable day in many respects, although we are advised against moving into a new house or changing our business address today. Travel is also considered to be contrary to the flow, so try to avoid long journeys if possible. An excellent day for local meetings and for getting together with friends, families and loved ones and if you have the urge to throw a party tonight, then go ahead because this is a very good time. Not only is the T'ung Shu in favour, but if you have been busy since the start of the Spring, then you have earned a little break and there is no better time for this than during the Earth season. Getting together with others always provides an opportunity to exchange ideas and opinions and during this phase of the year, when we are consolidating our position, a fresh insight can often help us identify the areas that we need to adjust in order to balance ourselves correctly.

Saturday April 22 – The Metal Dog – Essence of the day is Metal

A day of mixed blessings really, but a word of caution for those who get involved in conflict of any kind: the Almanac informs us that today there are no winners, only losers – unless you are a policeman or involved with law and order in some capacity, in which case, for today at least, the odds are stacked in your favour. If you find yourself in court for any reason and your cause is a just one, then take heart, because today the influences will enhance the ability of the court and all its officials to make a fair judgement on your behalf. It is easy to feel cynical about modern society, in which the bad guy is often seen to get away with it and the good guy sometimes has to take the blame, but today justice will be seen to be done.

Sunday April 23 – The Metal Pig – Essence of the day is Metal

Go with the flow today, because otherwise you will only invite trouble and if you feel like taking yourself off somewhere for the day, don't hesitate. Unfortunately, it is another one of those days when the Almanac advises us all to pack up and go fishing and this is really nature's way of telling us all to have a day off. It is important at any time to have some time to relax and unwind, but especially so at this time of the year when we need to prepare ourselves for an even more active period, the Summer. If things are flowing smoothly for you, then you should carry on, but if they are not, take some time off, chill out and go with the flow. As the Chinese proverb advises:

 When the wind blows, the grass bends.

Monday April 24 – The Water Rat – Essence of the day is Wood

An excellent start to the week and for those going back to work who heeded the advice of yesterday, they will no doubt be refreshed, and as a result they should be able to make full use of the opportunities that may well present themselves today. An active, inspiring day that will encourage everyone who tries to make the most from it, because this is the day of Ch'eng, a day of accomplishment and success. Clearly then, not a day to be idle, but a day to start implementing adjustments and changes in preparation for the Summer. Outside work is considered to be very favourable, so whether you are in or out of doors, at work or at home, there are no excuses and the onus is on everyone to make their contribution.

Tuesday April 25 – The Water Ox – Essence of the day is Wood

A very good day for business and trading in general, so whether you are buying or selling keep a look out for additional opportunities, because the indications are that these may well present themselves today. Respected Master T'ung informs us that this is the day of Shou, which is often regarded as meaning 'acceptance' or 'receiving' but it can also refer to gathering. For these reasons, it is also regarded as a very auspicious time to enter a college, university or some other institute of learning, in order to receive instruction, which, if initiated today, will produce very favourable results.

Wednesday April 26 – The Wood Tiger – Essence of the day is Water

Another very favourable day that encourages activity of all kinds, because everything is considered to be available today, so it would seem wise to keep your options open. When conditions are favourable, it encourages us to be more confident, which in turn inspires optimism, a necessary attribute at certain times, not least when we are beginning our journey. With Spring nearly at an end, we should have completed the first of our tasks for this year and although it has been very hectic at times, in many ways the activity of Summer is even greater. If there are any more openings that you would like to explore or anything new that you would like to consider, don't delay: use the beneficial influences of the day to support you.

Thursday April 27 – The Wood Rabbit – Essence of the day is Water

Today is the birthday of the goddess of the sea, Lin Ma-tzu, as she is known in Hong Kong and Macau, where great operas are staged in her honour today as a mark of gratitude. She was reputed to be a follower of Kuan Yin and legend has it that she is often seen by sailors and fishermen who are miraculously saved at sea. If you have a friend or loved one at sea today, light a candle in her honour and ask her to watch over them and protect them from danger. Good sentiments are to be encouraged today to balance out the negative ones which denote secret, underhand dealings, so take care because things are not always what they seem and it would be wise to keep in mind the Chinese proverb that says:

 Although he has seen a pig, he has never tasted pork.

Friday April 28 – The Fire Dragon – Essence of the day is Earth

The most positive aspects of today favour those who make a determined effort to prepare themselves for the immediate future. The T'ung Shu advises taking a look at the books today to chase up any unpaid accounts and also to settle any outstanding bills. Trading in general is fairly favourable, although the use of savings should be avoided if possible and it would also be wise not to dash around too much because travel is also not considered to be very auspicious. For those interested in the paranormal, the Constellation today is Kuei, often referred to as the Ghostly Carriage, and as a result there may be more activity in this department than usual and perhaps this may be a good night for spotting UFOs.

Saturday April 29 – The Fire Snake – Essence of the day is Earth

Feng shui remedies would be very favourable today because we are informed that this is the day for sweeping away negative influences of all kinds. This provides the perfect opportunity to clear the mind and pamper the body, which is just as important as cleaning the house or tidying the office. Fitness and health are both highlighted, so this is the perfect day to visit the gym, attend a t'ai chi class or enjoy a massage or anything else that takes your fancy. Rest, relaxation and recuperation should all be on the agenda today, and even if this entails spending a little time creating the right ambience for this to take place, at least you will be in harmony.

Sunday April 30 – The Earth Horse – Essence of the day is Fire

Family gatherings, meetings and conventions are all very well favoured today and as a result, anyone attending an exhibition or trade show should feel the benefit of additional inspiration from being in harmony with the day. This applies to everyone, irrespective of their role in the events, so whether it's business or pleasure, try to make the most of it; after all, the whole purpose is to have a good day. If you feel unfortunate because you are working when you would rather be playing, take a positive attitude, because if you can have a good day when you are working, then think how much fun you can have when it's time to play. We are reminded of this by the ancient Chinese sage, who said:

 Gems that are not worked form nothing useful.

Monday May 1 – The Earth Sheep – Essence of the day is Fire

Respected Master T'ung reminds us that today is associated with balance and harmony, the Chinese character P'ing, which can also be translated as 'peace and quiet'. Clearly today is not designed for an active start to the week, but as a period of transition, providing an opportunity to adjust and balance ourselves. This also applies to ideas and projects, so rather than proceeding full steam ahead today, perhaps it would be wise to take a step back and to try to look at things from a different perspective in order to see if there is anything else that could be done to improve the situation. Remember, Summer is nearly here and that will provide ample opportunity for even more activity, so enjoy the last few days of the Earth season and use it an an opportunity to check the compass and confirm your direction.

Tuesday May 2 – The Metal Monkey – Essence of the day is Wood

It is a pity that the portents are not more favourable for Geng Sheng day when the natural energy of the renewal cycle begins, but it would be wrong to expect everything to go our way and, as always, it is our duty to focus on the positive aspects. Keeping busy and staying active are the keys and by taking a cheerful and enthusiastic approach, you are less likely to be antagonistic and aggressive towards others. This approach may well pay dividends, because the T'ung Shu Almanac warns of dire consequences for those who make false accusations today. Preventative measures are often the best insurance, so for those who don't want to take any chances today, be like the Chinese proverb that says:

With bells on one's toes, there is a sound
with every step.

Wednesday May 3 – The Metal Rooster – Essence of the day is Wood

A beneficial day in many respects, although movement and travel in general are not considered to be very auspicious. There is a New Moon tomorrow, so it would be wise to keep this in mind today, because traditionally, during a time of no Moon, it was always considered prudent to remain still. A New Moon always brings a fresh burst of energy, so it would be better to postpone anything that would benefit from that, especially moving into a new home or new business premises, which we are advised to avoid today. The use of savings is also frowned upon, so clearly this is a day when we should be looking to consolidate our position, rather than looking at ways to exploit its potential.

Month 4

As always with a new lunar month, it begins on the day of the New Moon, although it would be wiser to consider today as Summer's eve as opposed to Summer's day. The indications are that Spring is not going to relinquish its position easily and as a result, there is a certain amount of conflict within the elements today. It is often said that New Moons are very good for making plans but not for carrying them out, and that is certainly the case today. The best advice is to get on with your life and ignore others, whose only object today may be to disrupt you. If you want to avoid any unnecessary hassle, keep this in mind and try not to react in a negative way, especially if you are faced with a difficult situation.

 It is useless to fight evil with evil; after all, even though the teeth are stronger, the lips last longer.

Today is the solar chi festival of Li Hsia, which marks the beginning of Summer, and this should bring about another change in the weather, hopefully for the better. Spring is still reluctant to relinquish its power so there is still an element of conflict in the air, but this will soon pass, so don't be too concerned. For many, today represents the end of the working week and it would be very sensible to use this as an opportunity to bring about the conclusion to the work of Spring in preparation for a new week and a new phase. Look at this coming weekend as a transitional period and any time that is devoted to contemplating the future is certain to bring about positive benefits.

Another day when it pays to go with the flow and if you are in the mood for a party, then you could do a lot worse than have one today. It does us all good to let our hair down now and again and sometimes it can motivate and inspire us at a later date; so if you feel the need to relax and chill out, spoil yourself and do just that. For those who may feel a little bit guilty at the prospect of having some time off purely for enjoyment, don't worry too much because with the arrival of Summer, there are going to be ample opportunities for plenty of hard work. That said, perhaps it would be wise for everyone to take a little break now, if only to store up vital energy in preparation for the onslaught of the Summer Fire.

Sunday May 7 – The Wood Ox – Essence of the day is Metal

An auspicious day for all kinds of activity, especially anything to do with the home, which is very appropriate for a Sunday when we should all try to spend at least some time with family, friends and loved ones. For those in the flow, eager to make use of the prospering Fire energy, this is a good day to exploit opportunities that may present themselves, but to expect maximum returns we should not be too eager. Summer has, after all, only just arrived and we should not expect too much too soon. If opportunities do present themselves, we should be grateful and accept them with gratitude and humility, even if they are not as lucrative as we would like.

It is foolish to allow the duck to escape by trying to catch the goose.

Monday May 8 – The Fire Tiger – Essence of the day is Fire

Summer is here and for many, it is the start of another week. Fortunately, it is considered to be reasonably favourable for trading and business in general, so we all have the opportunity to make a good start. The element of Summer is Fire, an activating, flourishing, upward energy, which is designed to make things grow and prosper, the natural step after the business of Spring when we plant seeds and instigate new growth. It is an active time, reaching its peak at the Summer solstice, and it is the time of year when the yang energy expands daily as the yin energy goes into decline. It would be wise to use the Summer energy to feed, nurture and encourage the growth of those plans, ideas and projects that were started in the Spring, thus keeping the flow going. It will take a little time for Summer to make its mark, so don't be too impatient as the Spring energy moves gradually into Summer.

Tuesday May 9 – The Fire Rabbit – Essence of the day is Fire

An active, encouraging day, which everyone should try to utilise to the best of their ability because it favours activity of all kinds. Respected Master T'ung informs us that it is the day of recuperation and anyone who has not been feeling their best recently should take heart because today the Heavenly Doctor is at work. If your doctor has not issued you with a sick note, then there are no excuses, because going with the flow today dictates that you use all your energy to nourish and feed your work, your dreams and your life. If you follow this advice today, you may be even more fortunate than you had hoped, because the Almanac also informs us that this is the day when treasure is uncovered, so, if you're feeling lucky, go for it.

Wednesday May 10 – The Earth Dragon – Essence of the day is Wood

A mixed day which may present a few obstacles, but nothing that cannot be overcome, so look at any potential stumbling blocks as challenges and imitate the action of Fire and rise up to them. The positive, beneficial influences will help to support those who adopt this attitude and if this involves contacting friends and supporters, then all the better, because these activities are considered to be very favourable today. Many people find it difficult to ask for help and support, even though they themselves may often help others, and this sometimes makes our lives more difficult than they need to be. So if you find it easy to give but difficult to receive, remember the Chinese proverb that says:

 If a horse does not enjoy wild grass, he will never grow fat and if a man receives no help, he cannot grow rich.

Thursday May 11 – The Earth Snake – Essence of the day is Wood

An excellent day which encourages good fortune in every respect, so not a day to miss out on, but one which should be used to the full. It is the day of Chien, a day to establish and a day in which it is said ten thousand things are generated, giving almost limitless potential. A great day to move into new premises, especially if the plans had been laid in the Spring. New partnerships and business of all kinds can flourish today, but only if you play your part by spending the day nurturing and attending to what needs to be done. The easiest time to do this is when the natural elements encourage it, so even if you don't really feel like making an effort, if you make a start, you may be surprised to find that things are a lot easier than you imagined.

Friday May 12 – The Metal Horse – Essence of the day is Earth

There will be a certain amount of depression in the atmosphere today, but this is only to be expected because once again the Constellation which represents the Ox Boy makes an appearance. It is a reminder of the sad separation that he and his lover, the Weaving Maiden, have to endure because of lack of balance. They were so in love that it is said they both neglected their duties and the maiden failed to weave any cloth and the Ox Boy neglected the herd. As a result, they were separated by the gods and banished to the Heavens where they were placed on either side of the Milky Way and they are only allowed to meet for one day each year. Respected Master T'ung suggests that we sweep away negative thoughts and ideas and anything else that acts as an obstacle to our progress, so clearly feng shui remedies would be very effective today, especially regarding our relationships.

Saturday May 13 – The Metal Sheep – Essence of the day is Earth

Another day of mixed blessings but one that favours matters relating to business rather than family gatherings, which may end in quarrels and arguments. If this does happen, try not to pay too much attention to them and use all your influence to ensure that they do not escalate into something much worse. Those at work are much more likely to have a good time because the energy is very conducive to making things happen, so it should be relatively easy to slip into a good routine today, especially if you have work to be getting on with. For those of you who are working and would prefer not to be, consider how fortunate you are to have the opportunity to achieve something instead of spending the day trying to avert conflict.

Sunday May 14 – The Water Monkey – Essence of the day is Metal

Another day which may encourage family disputes and if this happens, we are advised to take a balanced approach, because this would be in harmony with Respected Master T'ung. It is the day of P'ing, a time to balance, so meditation, personal cultivation and contemplation are all very much in the flow today. Other activities that are also designed to help us balance ourselves – like sound and colour therapy – would also be very appropriate today. If, on the other hand, you feel that all you need is a long walk with the dog, then don't hesitate, go with the flow, because today is not a day to deprive or deny yourself, it is a day when you give in and allow yourself to do whatever you feel like doing.

Monday May 15 – The Water Rooster – Essence of the day is Metal

Not a perfect start to the coming week although it could be a lot worse, but it would be wise for everyone to keep focused today: there may well be a lot of opportunities, but not all will be gateways to fortunate gardens. This should not prevent you from making the most of the favourable influences but it should prepare you by making you more aware. The worst thing you could do today would be to have unrealistic expectations, even if things do seem to be going incredibly well. Instead, enjoy the feeling that comes when things do go in your favour. Opportunities should be regarded as possibilities and not as instant solutions to problems, so keep in mind the Chinese proverb that says:

Pluck a feather from every passing goose,
but follow none.

Tuesday May 16 – The Wood Dog – Essence of the day is Fire

An auspicious day in many respects and certainly one that favours those who are active and attending to their duties. Domestic matters are considered to be particularly favourable today, so if you are stuck at home for any reason, don't take a negative approach to the work in hand; be positive and enthusiastic and you will get on much better. Outside activities are also considered to be in harmony and if you are lucky enough to have a garden and you don't feel like being inside, get out and cut the grass, tend to the plants or anything else you feel like doing. Presenting a pleasant face to the world is very good feng shui, so perhaps you could consider some tubs or containers with colourful, vibrant plants, placed near the entrance to help put a smile on the face of your house.

Wednesday May 17 – The Wood Pig – Essence of the day is Fire

Today marks the birthday of Lu Tung-pin, another one of the eight Heavenly Immortals, who is often associated with scholars, so if you are about to sit your exams, it would not do any harm to light a candle in his honour and ask him to support your efforts. Another legend associated with Lu T'ung-pin is that he was given a magic sword, which he used to slay wicked dragons, and it would be wise to remember this today, as a deterrent against conflict. This is the most negative aspect of the day, but you would be wise to stay clear of any confrontation, because you will only invite disaster. *The Art of War,* a book by Sun Tzu, has been studied by great military leaders for centuries and it contains information designed not only to win wars but also to avoid them. Sometimes we can win without even fighting and we should all keep in mind the words of Sun Tzu:

 If you wait by the banks of the river for long enough, eventually the bodies of your enemies will float past.

Thursday May 18 – The Fire Rat – Essence of the day is Water

Today is again the day of the Full Moon, when emotions may be running higher than usual, but if you are involved in any kind of litigation today, make sure that your argument has a sound basis and that it is not fuelled by personal desire. Failure to take this into account will only result in disaster today, because the energies are not conducive to supporting frivolous, petty actions. A day when, once again, it will pay to go with the flow and by taking an enthusiastic, almost carefree approach, you should have reasonable grounds to be fairly happy with the day's events.

Friday May 19 – The Fire Ox – Essence of the day is Water

Today provides the opportunity for everyone to finish this week on a high note, because all the portents indicate success in whatever you do. Activity of all kinds can flourish and prosper today and all we have to do to tap into this wonderful source of free energy is to flow with it. Long-distance travel is considered to be very beneficial, so if you are leaving today on business but you are unhappy at the prospect of being away from home, try to look on the bright side and consider the benefits that success usually brings. If you are attending an interview for a new job or you have a meeting with the bank manager or your boss, proceed with confidence, because, with the right attitude and a positive approach, you can achieve what you want today.

Saturday May 20 – The Earth Tiger – Essence of the day is Earth

Another very favourable day, especially for those in business, because the indications are that not only will the shops be busy but that people will be influenced to spend some of their savings, so clearly a good day for the retail sector. For the perfect day, try to avoid anything that involves too much travel, and if you do have to make a journey, then it would be prudent to allow plenty of time for delays. This is especially relevant to anyone who is getting married today, because, although you have selected a very auspicious day, if anything is going to go wrong, it will involve the transport side of things, so double-check the arrangements. If this is carried out, there should be no cause for concern as you are taking care of the most important element.

 The silkworm makes silk and the bee makes honey.

Sunday May 21 – The Earth Rabbit – Essence of the day is Earth

Today marks the solar chi festival of Hsiao Man, which relates to 'corn sprouting', meaning that the crops are beginning to flower and from now on the Summer energy really gathers momentum. This is the time when plans and projects that were started during the Spring can really take off and it is a time when we should push our ideas forward. With the positive, thriving Summer energy behind us, we can afford to promote ourselves with confidence, so put away the meek Spring-lamb outfit – it is time to roar like a tiger. If we use the active energy to help our hopes and dreams flourish, we improve our chances of a successful harvest in the Autumn. Today is also the birthday of the ruler of the Pole Star, one of the favourite deities of feng shui masters and astrologers, and if feng shui has made a positive improvement to your life, it would be wise to acknowledge this by lighting a candle in honour of the North Star and all the occupants of Heaven.

Monday May 22 – The Metal Dragon – Essence of the day is Metal

Today represents the perfect opportunity to turn negative into positive by using to your best possible advantage the beneficial aspects of what is otherwise a fairly unfavourable day. If you were waiting for an appropriate day to give up smoking, then consider doing it now, because along with other self-enforced regimes, these appear to have the biggest chance of success. Of course, you will still have to make an enormous effort, but if that is carried out at the appropriate time, then you can only improve your chances of success, which should provide enough motivation at least to consider it.

Tuesday May 23 – The Metal Snake – Essence of the day is Metal

A definite improvement on yesterday and, provided that your intentions are good, you have nothing to worry about. Business can prosper today, although the T'ung Shu Almanac advises taking a look at your finances rather than considering any further speculation, so clearly a day that favours credit control, including paying any outstanding bills that you may have overlooked. It's great to spend money, but sometimes we can derive an equally pleasing 'feel-good factor' by getting ourselves up to date. Even though paying bills is much less exciting than going shopping, it is all a question of balance and if we are normally late paying our rent, being on time can inspire us to be more responsible in future. Don't waste the day.

A foot of jade is of no value; an inch of time should be highly prized.

Wednesday May 24 – The Water Horse – Essence of the day is Wood

Feng shui remedies are again well favoured today, especially those implemented for business purposes. It would be wise to clear away any doubts and hesitations that you may feel and not to let them side-track you and disrupt your flow. If you are at work, take a good look around at your space and see if there is anything that is acting as an obstacle or barrier, preventing the beneficial energy from circulating. Every now and again, our desks get so overloaded, they resemble mountains and when this happens it is time for a clear-out – having a mountain on your desk only adds even more weight to your problems. Light and space are the two crucial factors and anything that you can do to to improve these aspects should be considered, because by improving your environment you improve the chances of flowing correctly and, more importantly, to your full potential.

79

Thursday May 25 – The Water Sheep – Essence of the day is Wood

A very favourable day to be involved with large or important events of any kind, irrespective of whether they are for business or pleasure. Very much a day to take part and participate in this favourable energy, not a day to observe others and drift around feeling sorry for ourselves. With the active Fire energy of Summer coupled with the favourable conditions of the day, this is a day when everyone can accomplish something; it only takes that initial effort. If you are unemployed and you are beginning to think that you will never find a job, put those ideas out of your head now, put on your best suit and your best smile and get out there. Get a local newspaper, go to the local job centre and ask around but, above all, do it with a positive frame of mind. Tell yourself that there is a job out there for you, all you need to do is find it.

Friday May 26 – The Wood Monkey – Essence of the day is Water

It is very appropriate that today is Friday, which for many people represents the end of the working week, because Respected Master T'ung reminds us that after the recent activity it is time to bring things to a conclusion and introduce a little more balance into our lives. This entails not taking our work home with us, so, if necessary, try to be a little more efficient than usual today and when it is time to go home, try to leave with a smile on your face. The weekend is coming, which should always provide some time for rest and recuperation, and the best advice is to go with the flow, look forward to it and above all, enjoy it.

 In all things success depends on preparation; without it, there is only failure.

Saturday May 27 – The Wood Rooster – Essence of the day is Water

Another active day that favours anything designed to make use of the prospering, active Summer energy. Outside activities are very favourable, so try to get out and about in the fresh air today and if you have entertainment on your mind, consider an outside event and start celebrating the fact that it is Summer. If your relationship has broken up recently and you still find it hard to adjust to being on your own, try to visit friends and family today and keep yourself occupied, because the negative aspects of the day are highlighted by the weeping willow. Distraction will work wonders today, so keep yourself busy and look forward to future prosperity and happiness.

Sunday May 28 – The Fire Dog – Essence of the day is Earth

The secret of success, as far as the Chinese are concerned, is all about making the best of your good luck and minimising the effects of your bad luck and if you were to follow this advice today, it would mean staying where you are. Not a good day to move into a new house, change your business premises, spend money that has been saved; even travel and physical movement in general are not advised. The good news is that you can put your feet up, relax and chill out. Don't even think about working all day in the garden, because even that is considered to be foolish; so don't fight it, go with the flow and have the day off.

Monday May 29 – The Fire Pig – Essence of the day is Earth

Today may well have its challenges – or perhaps I should say, you may well find others challenging you today – but either way, if you are prepared you should be able to cope easily. There will be many opportunities today but the chances are you will only be able to make use of these if you avoid conflict with others. The greatest chance of success will be in areas where there is no direct competition. This will enable you to work on your own, eliminating any chance of conflict with others who may have similar ambitions. It is difficult to agree to disagree even at the best of times, but today it would seem almost impossible to be able to achieve this with a friend, let alone a competitor, so keep in mind the Chinese proverb that says:

> Even friends should be separated by a high wall; it takes a superior man to avoid misunderstandings regarding business and money.

Tuesday May 30 – The Earth Rat – Essence of the day is Fire

There is a vast improvement today and the influences are much more favourable, which should encourage everyone, especially those who are working today. Although the emphasis has moved away from conflict, conditions are still not ideal and today should be viewed as a day to put things back on track, rather than going into overdrive. Very much a day to go with the flow because what works, works well, and what doesn't, probably won't at any cost; so save yourself the effort and focus on things that deserve your attention. There are times when however much we would like to influence a situation, we are unable to, and even though it hurts, we have to walk away and wait for another day.

Wednesday May 31 – The Earth Ox – Essence of the day is Fire

There is no need to have any reservations about today because the energy will encourage us all to be a lot more active and optimistic and hopefully, as a result, we should all be a lot happier today. Business matters are particularly favourable and the Almanac informs us that whatever is done on this day will bring great profit, but don't interpret this as a licence to do whatever you want. Use it to motivate you, safe in the knowledge that, for today at least, your efforts will be rewarded. Social occasions are also very much in harmony, but if you are attending a social function of any kind, try to keep things in moderation, especially alcohol, because if anything goes wrong today, it will be caused by careless talk. It is always good to enjoy ourselves and a perfect occasion concludes with a happy ending. It is the responsibility of everyone involved to ensure that this is the case, so keep in mind the Chinese proverb:

 One can never drink all the wine that is available.

Thursday June 1 – The Metal Tiger – Essence of the day is Wood

Another day when we should all be rushing to get out of bed as quickly as we can, because the possibilities are endless. Work, leisure, education, relationships and matters concerning the home are all favourable and the only thing that is considered taboo today is sitting around and doing nothing. This would be almost criminal – a flagrant waste of valuable energy and opportunity. The T'ung Shu is so confident that it even encourages the use of savings, if that is what it takes, so clearly there are no excuses and it's the responsibility of everyone to utilise this flourishing energy and to encourage others to do so as well. Remember, this is a time of expansion when ideas, hopes, dreams and plans can all prosper and if we do everything that we can, the chances are that these can all come to fruition, enhancing not only our own lives, but those of others as well.

Month 5

Friday June 2 – The Metal Rabbit – Essence of the day is Wood

With the month beginning on the day of the New Moon as usual, this is a good sign as new bursts of energy are always welcome, especially when we are active and therefore using up our resources. Today is also considered to be the birthday of the South Star of Longevity, one of the popular set of Three Figures that are so familiar in Chinese homes, businesses and restaurants. The other two figures represent wealth and happiness, but the South Star represents long life and he is the one who is often seen riding a deer, holding a peach and a staff, both symbols of longevity. Many people have these figures in their homes for good luck, but it would also be very good feng shui to light a candle and place it near them in honour of the occasion today.

Saturday June 3 – The Water Dragon – Essence of the day is Water

An inauspicious day in many respects: Respected Master T'ung informs us that today is closed for business. The Constellation doesn't help either, but we are encouraged to write letters and contact people, so if you enjoy surfing the Net, then today would be a good day to check your e-mail and use it either to promote yourself or as a source of inspiration for new ideas. Another positive aspect of the day is that it is a good time to collect and hoard things, and if you are attending a jumble sale or a garage auction, keep your eyes open, because the chances are something worthwhile may come to light.

Sunday June 4 – The Water Snake – Essence of the day is Water

All the negative energy is swept away today by very favourable conditions which encourage just about everything positive. This is a day when everything can flourish and offers an excellent opportunity to move up a gear to promote your ideas and hopes even more vigorously. It is a time to strive to greater heights, not an opportunity to waste by doing nothing, even if you are not at work today. Relationships, like everything else, need nourishment and encouragement in order to grow, and anything that is carried out today to promote this will certainly pay dividends in the future. Perhaps you should choose today to pamper your partner or a loved one or take the opportunity to treat the whole family and create a lovely memory that lasts a lifetime. Keep in mind the Chinese maxim that says:

 The family that stores up virtue will have an abundance of happiness.

83

Monday June 5 – The Wood Horse – Essence of the day is Metal

Today marks the solar chi festival of Mang Chung, which relates to the corn being in ear, the time when the crops begin to show themselves. This is a very active solar fortnight, ending with the Summer solstice, when the yang energy reaches its full power. At this time of the year it is important to remember that the yang energy is increasing daily and as the yang energy grows and the yin energy declines, the need for balance becomes even greater. Like yesterday, the portents are very favourable and this provides the perfect start to the working week which everyone should try to make use of. It's Summer, so be active, be happy and be confident.

Tuesday June 6 – The Wood Sheep – Essence of the day is Metal

Today is the day of the Dragon Boat Festival, one of the major Chinese festivals of the year celebrated by Chinese communities all over the world. Highly decorated, long, narrow rowing boats compete in races as a symbolic act of remembrance to Ch'u Yuan. He was a famous poet who is believed to have lived more than 2,000 years ago and legend has it that he drowned himself as a protest against a corrupt government. The fishermen at the time raced out in their boats in an attempt to save him, but his body was never found, and so now this re-enactment takes place every year to acknowledge his selfless action. Respected Master T'ung reminds us that today is the day for clearing away negative action and feng shui remedies are very much in harmony, especially if they are carried out in a sympathetic way that reflects the sacrifice made by Ch'u Yuan more than 2,000 years ago.

Wednesday June 7 – The Fire Monkey – Essence of the day is Fire

A day when nature gives everyone the green light, so don't have any doubts about today, especially if you are getting married – you have chosen a very auspicious day. Moving into a new home or new business, leaving on a business trip or attending an interview are all very much in the flow because things can be achieved today. Not a day to be timid but a day to be confident and to demonstrate your abilities and skills to others, so promote yourself as positively as you can as this will improve your chances of success. If your intentions are good, then you have nothing to worry about other than doing your best.

 Only life and death are predetermined; riches and honour depend on Heaven.

Thursday June 8 – The Fire Rooster – Essence of the day is Fire

Another very active day which favours those who are in the flow because today is only really an extension, carrying on from where we left off yesterday. This is another excellent opportunity to make good use of this prospering Summer energy to promote ourselves, our ideas and our work and to project ourselves in the best possible way. It is a time to chase things up, push things along and to encourage and inspire others, who all play their part. It is not a time to let off steam but a time to commit our energy to those causes which were started in the Spring, and from which we will be looking to harvest rewards in the Autumn.

Friday June 9 – The Earth Dog – Essence of the day is Wood

It would be wise to keep yourself busy today, especially if you are separated from your partner for any reason, because once again the Ox Boy makes an appearance today, which does put a bit of a wet blanket on the proceedings, as we are reminded of his sadness. As always, it is better to focus on the more positive aspects, which include activity of all kinds, especially any work that is carried out in the garden, which would benefit from your attention today. Have a look around the outside of the house and see what can be done to brighten it up and make it look and feel happier, because it is important to project a bright and enthusiastic appearance.

Saturday June 10 – The Earth Pig – Essence of the day is Wood

If you have the opportunity to stay at home today, then consider yourself fortunate because, for today at least, this is where the action is. Domestic activity is considered very important, but once that is out of the way, if you feel like inviting some friends round and having a small party, then don't hesitate. We all spend a lot of time and effort trying to make our homes feel warm and inviting, but we don't often get the opportunity to invite our friends and family over; so if you feel that you need an excuse, today you have one – it's called going with the flow. Remember, however, the Chinese proverb that says:

 Let idlers remain outside the home but encourage
the virtuous to enter.

Sunday June 11 – The Metal Rat – Essence of the day is Earth

After the positive, joyous influences of yesterday, it's no surprise to receive the opposite sentiments today because this is the yin and yang of life. If we are aware of negative forces, it is much easier to avoid them, and that is what today should be all about: not seizing opportunities but avoiding obstacles. Everything points to a day of conflict, quarrels and confrontation, so clearly it is not going to be an easy day, not least of all for the children who may find themselves at odds with their parents. If this is the case and you are having difficulty with your parents, keep in the mind the Chinese proverb that tells us:

Keep your parents warm in the Winter, but cool in the Summer.

Monday June 12 – The Metal Ox – Essence of the day is Earth

After an unfavourable day, there is usually an improvement and this is certainly the case today, although it is still a day when it would be wise not to expect too much. If you go with the flow, you should be fine; this is very much the characteristic of the day and what flows, flows well – but as for the rest of it, well, forget it. There is very little that can be done to make something work that doesn't want to, and that includes people, ideas and dreams as well as machinery and animals, so this is not a day to force issues of any kind. Even gentle persuasion would be futile today and you are far better off leaving it all for another day and just letting today happen in its own way.

Tuesday June 13 – The Water Tiger – Essence of the day is Metal

The week can really take off now, because today provides very favourable conditions for everyone, whether they are at home or at work. For those in business, today encourages any activity that is designed to help the business grow and expand, and new directions, promotions or campaigns are all very well favoured. Building, construction and new ventures in general are also considered fortunate, so much so that the Almanac advises us that the Emperor himself will bestow his blessings on our ventures today. With the royal seal of approval, it is difficult to see where we could go wrong, so avoid the obvious mistake which would be to miss out completely by not participating.

Wednesday June 14 – The Water Rabbit – Essence of the day is Metal

Today is the birthday of Kuan P'ing, who is the patron of martial arts and whose image is used to remind students that strength must never be abused. If you attend any classes in the martial arts, t'ai chi or other related styles of self-empowerment, it would be very good feng shui to acknowledge his birthday today and light a candle in his honour as a sign of respect. A favourable day that encourages activity of all kinds, especially business and trading in general, and a time when it is even considered fairly safe to open up the treasuries and delve into savings. Of course, balance is still the key, so don't use this as an excuse to go on a spending binge, but as long as you are sensible, you should finish the day in profit.

Thursday June 15 – The Wood Dragon – Essence of the day is Fire

A day that favours music as well as the arts, so anyone involved in these pursuits will certainly benefit from additional inspiration today. This applies to everyone who participates, so whether you are a performer or a spectator, you are likely to enjoy yourself even more than usual. Respected Master T'ung also informs us that it is the day of recuperation, which should encourage anyone who may have been feeling under the weather recently and not at their best. For those at work, a day when you should consider finishing the jobs in hand rather than tackling new ones and you are also advised to take a look at the accounts to make sure there are no nasty surprises. Not an exciting day, but the sort of day where it would be wise to pay attention to detail: if there is anything out of place, you are sure to notice.

Friday June 16 – The Wood Snake – Essence of the day is Fire

Today is the day of the Full Moon, which may well account for any unpredictable behaviour. Emotions always run higher during this time as the Moon expands to its full force, but today the elements are very much in conflict and, as a result, this is a day to be particularly careful. Even the portents cannot agree, because on the one hand there appear to be opportunities, but on the other we are informed that the 'shops are closed'. Perhaps it would be best to be prudent, and if you come across opportunities today, restrict yourself to looking at them; if the goods are still available when the shop is open and you still want them, look at them again. Whatever you do, don't let your heart go running away, fuelled by emotion that may well not be there for very long. Remember the Chinese proverb that says:

 The heart is like running a horse on a level plain, easily loosed, but very difficult to restrain.

Saturday June 17 – The Fire Horse – Essence of the day is Water

Today is the festival of Heaven and Earth, from which, it is said, came yin and yang and thence the four seasons, the five elements and all of creation. It is also the birthday of Tathagata Buddha. At the head of Buddhist gods in China, there are the Three Precious Ones, representing Buddha, the Law and the Church. Tathagata Buddha is the head of the Church and as such, he is seen as Gautama, the prince who founded the Buddhist faith. An auspicious day, then, and one when we should celebrate and give thanks for the success that we do enjoy in life and not dwell on our failures. It also goes without saying that if you have any statues or figures of Buddha in the home or at work, you should light a candle or place some flowers there today, because it would be very bad to ignore his birthday.

Sunday June 18 – The Fire Sheep – Essence of the day is Water

Sporting activities are very much in harmony today and whether you decide to go jogging, swimming or just lazing around in the sauna, you can justify it all by going with the flow. Space-clearing is also considered very favourable today, especially if this is being carried out to clear away negative, stagnant energy, caused perhaps by a broken relationship. The Constellation is very much in harmony with Respected Master T'ung today, represented by the weeping willow, so the best course of action would be to sweep it all away and clear out any obvious reminders. Try to focus on positive aspects regarding health and use them as an excuse to spoil yourself with a session of your favourite remedy, whatever that happens to be.

Monday June 19 – The Earth Monkey – Essence of the day is Earth

Another birthday today, this time of the Old Royal Mother, who is said to attend to the peach orchard where the peaches of immortality are grown. This is clearly a very responsible job and it is not surprising that she is associated with longevity and is said to have the power to grant long life. A useful lady to know then, and so, if you are not already familiar with her, get to know her today by lighting a candle in honour of her birthday. A very auspicious day which favours big events of all kinds: don't ignore it, don't waste it and above all, don't abuse it by trying to monopolise it; it belongs to everyone.

Tuesday June 20 – The Earth Rooster – Essence of the day is Earth

It would be good to relax a bit today. If you are still in full flow from yesterday, then you should not encounter any difficulties, but otherwise it would be a good time to wind down. Respected Master T'ung reminds us that it is the day of balance and therefore a good time to sit back and contemplate our position rather than advancing ahead regardless. It is nature's way of providing a coffee break, allowing us to have a little time to adjust ourselves during what is a very hectic period of the year. We find it difficult to accept sometimes that we cannot achieve something every day, but that is just not possible within the natural cycle of things and it would go completely against the principles of yin and yang. As the Chinese proverb says:

 Forcing the crops makes a dull market.

Wednesday June 21 – The Metal Dog – Essence of the day is Metal

Today marks the solar chi festival of Hsia Chih, which relates to the Summer solstice, an important marker in the Chinese calendar, denoting a major turning point in the year. Today is yang energy at its greatest before it begins to decline towards its weakest point at the Winter solstice. Conversely, the levels of yin energy have now reached their weakest point. An important day then and one to acknowledge and use, because a great deal can be achieved with so much yang energy floating around. The worst thing that you could do is to sit around feeling sorry for yourself, because the energy is there to help you, but if you don't get out there and grab a piece of the action for yourself, how can you expect to improve your life?

Thursday June 22 – The Metal Pig – Essence of the day is Metal

Today is not a good day to be dashing about all over the place; travel in general is not considered very favourable, so try to stay close to home if possible. Domestic activity is very well favoured, both inside and outside the home, so it would be a good idea to make use of the Summer energy and try to find jobs in the garden to complete. We are also advised to resist the urge to shop, because this may well involve additional unforeseen expenses that will put a damper on the day, because today is clearly a day when money could get out of control. The Fire energy of Summer, coupled with the portents influencing the energy of the day, could all combine, resulting in your spending a lot more than you had planned, so be warned and if you have to go shopping, leave the plastic at home.

FENG SHUI ALMANAC 2000

Friday June 23 – The Water Rat – Essence of the day is Wood

Not a day which really encourages positive actions because the influences favour more negative traits, so a good day to take control and exercise integrity, restraint and an unbiased attitude towards others. Conflict is in the air again, as Respected Master T'ung reminds us, but this time it is blended with the Constellation representing the Ghostly Carriage, denoting conflict even within the spirit world. A good day to exercise caution and to keep a low profile, especially if you are contemplating anything that might clash with the law, because today, the odds are very much in favour of the police force and authority in general. The best advice would be to keep in your place, because as the Chinese proverb tells us:

 The serpent knows his own hole.

Saturday June 24 – The Water Ox – Essence of the day is Wood

Although today is more favourable than yesterday, it would be wise to take a light-hearted view of any obstacles that may present themselves. It is a day when going with the flow offers the only possibility of achieving anything worthwhile. There are other options, of course, if you like banging your head against a wall, but if you want a headache you might be better to consider a hangover instead and have a party tonight. You may wish to walk up a mountain but rather than attempt it with the wind against you, postpone it until the wind is in your favour and today, unfortunately, it is not. However inconvenient that may be, the best thing to do is to accept it.

Sunday June 25 – The Wood Tiger – Essence of the day is Water

A favourable day in many respects, which encourages everyone to go about their business freely, especially as travel is also considered to be fairly favourable. That makes it a good day to enjoy ourselves, but we should bear in mind the fact that Respected Master T'ung advises us all to avoid gossiping and especially to refrain from making any derogatory statements about others. This will not be tolerated today and failure to heed this advice may result in dire consequences for those who ignore it.

Monday June 26 – The Wood Rabbit – Essence of the day is Water

An excellent start to the week that should encourage everyone in their efforts, so not a day to miss out on, because with such favourable energy, everyone can prosper. Business and trading in general could be very profitable, as one of the aspects of the Constellation is associated with the thriving, industrious silkworm. Academic matters are also very well favoured and anyone taking an examination today has every reason to feel confident, provided they have made use of their time appropriately. If you are studying, try to focus on what you are doing and, more importantly, on your attitude to study and learning in general. Remember, it is important to learn the basic concepts of the subject you are studying and often, to do that effectively, you need to think clearly.

 Clear knowledge is more valuable than profound knowledge.

Tuesday June 27 – The Fire Dragon – Essence of the day is Wood

You may find this a day of mixed fortunes but with the right attitude and a positive approach, there are always things that can be achieved. We are reminded to attend to letters and other correspondence today, but this should be carried out in a positive way, so don't look at it as a chore, look at it as another opportunity to promote yourself. With the active, expanding energy of Summer to support you, this is the perfect time to make your plans and projects blossom and start to bear fruit and the best way to achieve that is to feed and encourage them. It is very important that you fully believe in what you are doing, but if you are committed and your intentions are good, then at least you have half a chance, which improves, of course, as you learn to go with the flow.

Wednesday June 28 – The Fire Snake – Essence of the day is Wood

Today has an interesting blend of influences but everything points to confusion, and as a result you may find yourself wondering whether you are coming or going. If half of you wants to conquer the world today, but the other half wants to stay in bed, don't worry too much – it is that sort of day. If you are at work, try to slip into a nice, safe routine and have a quiet day, attending to the less demanding, more mundane aspects of your work. If you are at home, don't set yourself any targets because that will only put additional pressure on you. That's the last thing you need, so if the weather is nice, try to spend as much time outside as possible – and relax.

Thursday June 29 – The Earth Horse – Essence of the day is Fire

We have a very auspicious combination of influences today, ideal for anyone who wishes to make use of them. New ventures of any kind are particularly favourable, so if you are moving into new premises, taking on a new partner or striking out in a new direction, you certainly have the force behind you today. Business prospects look very good and you must stay focused and alert, because although opportunities will present themselves, the onus is on you to spot them, so leave the radar switched on. Respected Master T'ung also reminds us to leave our savings where they are, so this is not a day to profit purely from speculation but a day when hard work and a keen eye are the routes to success.

Friday June 30 – The Earth Sheep – Essence of the day is Fire

Feng shui is again very well favoured today, as we are reminded to have our regular clean-up of mind, body and spirit, as well as our space. That makes it a good time to sweep away doubts, fears and obstacles which prevent us from moving forward in a positive way. If you are feeling tired and jaded, then you need to rejuvenate the body as well as the mind, so treat yourself to one of the many therapies that are designed to do just that. If your mind is cluttered and full to bursting point, then you have to look at ways to relieve the mental stress. Consider meditation or a session in a flotation tank, or whatever else takes your fancy. The important thing is to use today as an opportunity to eliminate doubt and hesitation and by doing so, improve your confidence and determination, necessary attributes if you are going to thrive and prosper during this Summer.

Saturday July 1 – The Metal Monkey – Essence of the day is Wood

The influences today are not in harmony and this is certain to cause conflict somewhere, although it should be fairly easy to avoid. Travel by sea is not considered favourable because the Almanac warns that there is a possibility of being shipwrecked today, although other modes of transport do not appear to be affected, so leave the yacht in the marina and take the plane instead. If you are caught in a difficult financial position, it would be wise to be realistic and practical, because it will not help to juggle things around too much in the expectation of something else happening. Be optimistic, be confident but also keep in mind the Chinese proverb that warns us:

 Don't steal the cat's meat to feed the dog.

Month 6

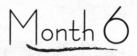

A new lunar month, a New Moon to provide a fresh burst of energy, and the Birthday of Wei T'o, who is often seen guarding Buddhist temples and who looks after us all. Respected Master T'ung encourages personal cultivation today, so it would be wise to consider taking some time out for meditation and quiet meditative thought in order to balance our minds. This is traditionally a day of fasting for Buddhists, so going with the flow today does not entail rushing around at the speed of light. Try to slow down and absorb the subtle but beneficial energy that the New Moon always brings. Harmony is the name of the game and following nature's natural energy cycles is the first step. Consider the Chinese proverb:

 Dogs watch by night; the cock announces the dawn.

A good day to try to keep busy and although it is not the perfect start to the week, don't use it as an excuse to do nothing, because on days like today it is even more important to make an effort. Outside work is very favourable, so working in the garden is in harmony, and since it is Summer and the weather is probably good, this would seem to be the best advice. If you are unable to do this and you find yourself stuck in an office, don't be negative. Treat yourself to a nice flowering house plant and place it near to where you sit as a symbolic act of bringing Summer into your space.

There is no doubt today about the beneficial influences, of which there are plenty, so not a day to be idle but one to harness the favourable aspects and make them work for you. Domestic activity is considered very favourable and those who are at home today will probably get the best deal – bettered only by those who work from home. Not a day for dashing about but one for attending to matters closer to home, so tonight would be a great time for the family to get-together. Perhaps it would be a good idea to consider a barbecue to inspire you to spend a few hours tidying up the garden, something which the Almanac also considers to be very much in harmony today.

Wednesday July 5 – The Wood Rat – Essence of the day is Metal

If you can avoid the negative aspects of the day, you can certainly benefit, especially if you are using the Summer energy correctly and you are encouraging your ideas and plans to expand and flourish. The Almanac informs us that if we push open new doors today, we can double our good fortune and that will provide an even greater incentive to try to exploit any opportunities that may come our way. Balance is the key, because it is also important to take the negative aspects into account and these reflect confrontation and conflict. If you find yourself competing with others today, keep this in mind and don't allow the desire to succeed to bring out the negative aspects of your character. Keep in mind the Chinese proverb:

When the gains are great, the losses are correspondingly heavy.

Thursday July 6 – The Wood Ox – Essence of the day is Metal

Another good day to focus on what is positive and to avoid getting caught by negative influences, although it is important to stress that the emphasis today is on the word favourable. Not a day for hesitation then, and if you are selective and you avoid things that are particularly difficult, you can achieve a lot. This would be a good day to switch into 'automatic pilot' mode so that you can attend to your tasks efficiently, methodically and without any fuss. If you are stuck at home today, the Almanac reminds us that it is an excellent day for physical labour, so if the weather is good, try to get outside and do some work on the house or in the garden.

Friday July 7 – The Fire Tiger – Essence of the day is Fire

Today marks the solar chi festival of Hsiao Shu, which means 'little heat', and this denotes the beginning of the last month of Summer. Although we have already had the Summer solstice, the yang Fire energy is still very active and a lot of this energy has been 'stored' to be released over the next month. It is very important at this time to monitor your 'crops', so anything that you can do to add nourishment to feed your ideas, plans and projects will pay dividends in the Autumn. This really cannot be stressed too much. If you plant your aspirations and dreams in the Spring, then nurture and nourish them in the Summer, you can expect a reasonable harvest, at the very least, in the following Autumn.

Saturday July 8 – The Fire Rabbit – Essence of the day is Fire

A fortunate day in many respects, especially for those leaving on holiday today because the influences favour long-distance travel. It is true that patience may be pushed to the limit but that is a small price to pay for a holiday that has the blessings of the Emperor. Outside activities are also considered good today, so whether you are at work, at home or at play, there is no excuse for failing to make an effort to energise yourself into action and enjoy the favourable conditions. Failure to heed this advice will only result in wasted opportunities and it would be much smarter to grab them while you can. If you miss the chance, the Chinese proverb reminds us of the consequences.

 Spilt water is much harder to gather.

Sunday July 9 – The Earth Dragon – Essence of the day is Wood

There is a conflict of interests again today, so it will pay to remain positive and focused, because it is certain there will be more than a few distractions. The secret of today is to support your own interests and avoid getting caught up in somebody else's slipstream. Study and education are very well favoured and if you find yourself with a mountain of homework, don't panic: arrange it into some sort of order, then decide what to do first. It sounds too good to be true, but if you organise yourself in such a way that you feel comfortable and you make an effort – especially if you can have the Grand Duke in the east supporting you as you have today – the daily influences will be working for you and not against you and this will improve your output and sense of overall achievement.

Monday July 10 – The Earth Snake – Essence of the day is Wood

Respected Master T'ung advises us that today is the day of recovery when the messenger of Heaven's Emperor recovers, no doubt aided by the visit of the Heavenly Doctor who is said to attend to everyone today. If you have a friend or loved one who is recovering from illness, send them a message of encouragement to help their recuperation. This would enhance the beneficial aspects of the day and provide a feel-good factor that everyone can thrive on. This is arguably the best fuel to make use of, especially when we are all attempting to fire up our plans, hopes and aspirations and trying to encourage others to participate in our projects.

Tuesday July 11 – The Metal Horse – Essence of the day is Earth

It may be difficult to get into the flow today because the energy is not exactly conducive for that; in fact, it is rather closed down. This is in contradiction to the information we have that the Emperor himself bestows his blessings on those whose initiate new ventures today – a good example of how the principles of yin and yang affect our daily lives. In this case the yin, or negative aspect, is that the conditions are not very favourable but the yang, or positive aspect, is that if you can make it today, then you will make it 'big-time'. In a way, this makes it a bit of an all-or-nothing day and the smart thing to do is to expect nothing, but try your best anyway. That way, you should find yourself in a win-win situation.

Wednesday July 12 – The Metal Sheep – Essence of the day is Earth

There is no confusion today because it appears to be auspicious in every respect, which should encourage a positive attitude from everyone and motivate us all to try to utilise the energies to the best of our abilities. With the exception of opening our treasuries – a reference to using our savings – everything seems favourable, especially trading and business, so whatever you are selling, go with the flow and enjoy yourself. Of course this works both ways and you may find yourself the target of some pretty convincing sales talk, but as long as you remember that the bank is closed today and you don't commit yourself, you should survive. If you meet an expert sales operator, then remember the Chinese proverb that warns us against such people:

 He has the legs of a dancer and the mouth
of a storyteller.

Thursday July 13 – The Water Monkey – Essence of the day is Metal

A day which favours feng shui remedies, health and fitness regimes and cleansing in general, so not a day to be negative. If you are feeling a bit that way inclined, then use your favourite therapy, whatever that is, to snap out of it. Negative thoughts, feelings and ideas should all be swept away and not allowed to take root, because they will disrupt your flow long after they have passed on. At this time of year, when activity can sometimes appear to be out of control, it is a good idea to take a little time out now and again to clear away the debris as we produce it. Clutter can build up surprisingly quickly and it is important to keep on top of it and not be overwhelmed by it. Look at it as 'debris control'! Because we produce so much of it – physical, emotional and spiritual – it needs to be monitored on a regular basis.

Friday July 14 – The Water Rooster – Essence of the day is Metal

Today is the birthday of Lu Pan, the imperial carpenter who is also the patron saint of builders. It is said that he was born more than 2,500 years ago and when he retired, he lived as a hermit and learned the skills of magic and produced wonderful machines and inventions. The invention of the feng shui ruler is often attributed to him. This ruler denotes favourable dimensions for beds, tables, windows, doors and anything to do with the house. To the Chinese, proportion and size must be in harmony and certain combinations are considered to be more favourable than others. In the West, we are very familiar with the various paper sizes used in stationery – A3, A4, A5 and so on – but very few people think of their proportions as Chinese. However, it was the Chinese who conceived the measurements as they realised that these were the only sizes that could be folded in half and yet would still retain the original proportions. Think about that the next time you doubt the wisdom of the ancient Chinese.

Saturday July 15 – The Wood Dog – Essence of the day is Fire

This is a very auspicious day to get married, because the Almanac informs us that children born of a marriage that takes place today will always have money in their pockets, which is not exactly the biggest handicap with which to burden your future children. Large events of all kinds are favoured today, irrespective of whether they are for business or pleasure, so if you have an important meeting planned, you can relax as you are in the flow. Job interviews are particularly favourable as well, so don't be nervous, the only thing to worry about is not turning up. Not a day for tackling petty tasks, but a day to go for it big-time and make a difference.

Sunday July 16 – The Wood Pig – Essence of the day is Fire

Another good day to keep active, especially in the garden, because the Almanac approves of this today, so if the weather is nice, don't stay indoors, get out and absorb the active Summer energy. If you are feeling a little jaded, don't worry too much because the Earth season will be here again soon, which will provide everyone with an opportunity to take a little time out to adjust and balance themselves. In the meantime, we need to try to make use of the favourable conditions in order to nourish and nurture our hopes and dreams by promoting ourselves and our ideas in the most positive, enthusiastic way. There is always something we can do, as the Chinese proverb tells us:

A man is not like a utensil, which has only specific and limited uses.

Monday July 17 – The Fire Rat – Essence of the day is Water

A very auspicious day today for those in business because the portents indicate that this is a day when things can be accumulated, so any effort made today should certainly bring benefits. This should encourage those who are looking to push their projects into another phase, or who have been waiting for the right conditions to expand; so be confident and enthusiastic because this is a day when your aspirations can flourish and grow. Domestic activity is also very favourable, so if you are stuck at home for any reason, try to find something constructive to do to make yourself feel you are contributing. Travel is not particularly auspicious and Respected Master T'ung also warns us against unnecessary expenditure and although it is not a bad day to acquire a new house, it is not advisable to move into it today.

Tuesday July 18 – The Fire Ox – Essence of the day is Water

It may be difficult to go with the flow today because all the indications point to a day of conflict, which will unfortunately have a bad influence on some people. The secret today is to avoid putting yourself in a position where these influences can affect you, but if that is not possible, then you have to conduct yourself accordingly. It is not always easy to walk away from conflict and sometimes, in our business dealings or more commonly in our relationships, we are confronted with conflict whether we like it or not. When we find ourselves in this position, we have no option but to deal with it, and at that point we often react in a negative way. If you find yourself in this position, remember that balance and harmony are essential and keep in mind the words of Confucius:

> The superior person promotes unity and does not perpetrate differences. Petty people compare themselves with each other, which destroys unity.

Wednesday July 19 – The Earth Tiger – Essence of the day is Earth

Although today represents an improvement on yesterday, it would be wise to approach it with a sense of humour, because otherwise you may only end up in tears. The Earth season begins tomorrow and this last day of the Fire period represents a challenging aspect that it would be wise not to ignore. This is best achieved by going with the flow and not forcing issues of any kind, especially with your partner, because nothing of any worth can be achieved today. Consider this a day to put everything behind you and slip into a nice, safe routine even if that involves finding a comfortable chair and losing yourself in a good book or anything else that keeps you happy.

Thursday July 20 – The Earth Rabbit – Essence of the day is Earth

Today marks the beginning of the Summer Earth season, the second of the four Earth seasons that occur during the course of the year. During this time, it is good to balance and adjust ourselves after the activity of the Summer Fire, arguably the most energetic time of year, in order to realign ourselves in preparation for the coming Autumn. Today offers the ideal conditions to consolidate our position and to do anything that is needed to make sure that our hopes and plans are on course and moving in the right direction. It is important to remember that Autumn is approaching. This is a time of harvest, but the more work we put in now, the better that will be. This period provides an ideal opportunity for a final look at what we are doing in order to see if we can make any last-minute improvements; it would be a pity to waste it.

Friday July 21 – The Metal Dragon – Essence of the day is Metal

Today should provide an opportunity for a prosperous end to the week, and those in business should keep this in mind and apply themselves fully to the tasks in hand. Students should also try to utilise these favourable conditions because the daily influences also favour anyone studying, entering a new college or sitting an examination of any kind. Conditions for trading, dealing and exchanging are all very favourable today and the only cause for concern, as the Almanac informs us, is travel, which should be avoided if possible. If this is not possible, then allow plenty of time for the journey, because there are bound to be delays and congestion.

Saturday July 22 – The Metal Snake – Essence of the day is Metal

Today marks the solar chi festival of Ta Shu, which translates as 'great heat' and this represents the last solar fortnight of Summer. Don't let this depress you because Autumn can be very active and rewarding, so there is plenty to look forward to. In the meantime, there is no time to dwell on anything negative, so make the most of the Summer energy while it's here. Remember, this is a time when your hopes can flourish and it is the perfect opportunity to push your ideas and plans forward, so be confident and optimistic, and above all, try to be happy within yourself. Promote yourself in a positive way, but keep in mind the words of Confucius, who said:

 Do not preach what you practise, until you have practised what you preach.

Sunday July 23 – The Water Horse – Essence of the day is Wood

Perhaps it would be wise to consider spending the day at home if possible, and taking the day off; this is what nature is doing today, so we may as well follow suit. Relaxation is the order of the day, although entertaining at home would also be very appropriate, especially if this is kept to small, intimate groups. However active you feel, you should keep in mind the fact that the market might not be open so there is no point in trying to chase opportunities that don't exist, even if there are others who are convinced they do.

> Beware of the fish dealer who has not brought his basket, because although he hooks with his mouth, he has no fish.

Monday July 24 – The Water Sheep – Essence of the day is Wood

An excellent start to the week and one that should enable us all to slip into a harmonious routine that can help to set the standard for the coming week. Today encourages us to make a start in our preparations for Autumn and to consider what changes this will bring and how we can best adjust ourselves to suit. If you have made the most from Spring and you have devoted the Summer to promoting and expanding those things that were started, you have a very active Autumn to look forward to, in which case the more prepared you are, the more successful you will be. The harvest is only a reflection of the work put in by the farmer with the additional blessing of nature, and if you have put your work in, you have every reason to be optimistic.

> When buying a horse from the manger, first look at its mother.

Tuesday July 25 – The Wood Monkey – Essence of the day is Water

Today is the birthday of K'uan Ti, the god of war, who is regarded as the chief supporter of Heaven and the protector of the kingdom. He is thought to have lived more than 2,000 years ago and there are many stories and legends concerning him, but in 1594, during the Ming dynasty, the Emperor Wan Li proclaimed him a god. At one time there were thousands of temples all over China dedicated to him and it is important to stress that he is seen as having the power to avert war and to be able to protect people from the horrors that war always produces. The influences today encourage sweeping away negative energy, so it would be good feng shui to start by lighting a candle in honour of K'uan Ti and asking him to support you in your efforts.

Wednesday July 26 – The Wood Rooster – Essence of the day is Water

A very good day to slip into top gear because all the indications are that this is a day of success. Weddings are particularly favourable, because we are reminded that children born of a marriage conducted today will become highly accomplished and talented – not a bad start in life! Meetings, conventions and conferences are all very well favoured and today is the perfect time for an interview, and any job secured today will certainly bring much in the way of future prosperity. With Autumn just around the corner, this is a perfect opportunity to look around and see if there is anything else that you can do to encourage a successful harvest.

Thursday July 27 – The Fire Dog – Essence of the day is Earth

Another very encouraging day that we should all try to use to our advantage. If you are still busy with the events of yesterday, the way forward is clear, because there is nothing to prevent you from continuing the good work. If you have concluded yesterday's business, then it would be a good idea to take stock of your situation today rather than go dashing around looking for new opportunities. Balance is the key and since this is the Summer Earth season, it would be wise to use this opportunity to make any adjustments that may be necessary to enable you to get back on track. Summer is coming to an end and it would be a good idea to start thinking about Autumn, because the quicker you can adjust, the less time you will lose and when the harvest is good, there is no time to waste. After all:

 Where there is great merit, there is great reward.

Friday July 28 – The Fire Pig – Essence of the day is Earth

An appropriate opportunity for those in business to end the week on a flourishing note; the positive aspects of the daily influences will encourage this, provided of course that they stay enthusiastic and positive. Outside activities are also considered to be favourable so if you are stuck at home, try to get outside and absorb the Summer energy. Gardening and attending to pots and planters would very much be in the flow and, that being the case, perhaps you should consider giving the outside of the house a facelift. Much of the beneficial chi enters the home through the windows. It is fundamental for good feng shui to keep windows clean and sparkling to encourage the favourable yang energy to enter, and it is important to replace any glass that is cracked, as in feng shui terms this distorts the chi as it passes through.

Saturday July 29 – The Earth Rat – Essence of the day is Fire

If you are looking for an opportunity to stay at home to catch up with a few things you haven't had time for, then today looks like a good prospect. Adjustment often involves additional activity in order to finish off tasks that have not been completed and with the right attitude today you can make progress in that area in leaps and bounds. Respected Master T'ung advises us that it would not be wise to move into a new home today, because travel is not considered very auspicious. As always, it pays to know these things in advance, so if you are faced with the prospect of travelling somewhere today, allow plenty of time because things might not flow the way that you would like them to and you could encounter difficulties or delays.

Sunday July 30 – The Earth Ox – Essence of the day is Fire

Not surprisingly, some of the aspects encourage negativity as this is the last day of this lunar month and a time when there is no influence from the Moon, often associated with secret, underhand dealings. The Almanac warns us to avoid conflict today because quarrels and arguments will only escalate into something that everyone will have cause to regret. A positive and cheerful approach is what is needed at times like this, because it is the only effective remedy against negative influences. You may be confronted by a friend or loved one today and it is important not to react in a negative way, so listen to them and try to understand their point of view. It would be wise to try to resist the temptation to put your own views across too strongly because this is a day that favours only one person at a time; otherwise the chances are that it will end on a negative note. Consider the words of Confucius and try to take this approach today.

Do not worry about not being understood, but be concerned that you understand others.

Month 7

Monday July 31 – The Metal Tiger – Essence of the day is Wood

This month's New Moon heralds the birthday of Tai Shung Lao-chun, or Lao Tzu as he is more commonly known, the founder of Taoism who remains a central figure in Taoist thought and philosophy. He is often depicted as an old man riding a buffalo, and figures and statues of him are common in traditional Chinese households. If you have one of his figures in your home or at work, it would be very appropriate to light a candle in his honour today as a mark of respect to this great philosopher. He continues to have a positive influence on those seeking the meaning of life, and as the founder of Taoism ('the way') and author of such classics as the *Tao Teh Ching*, he remains a valuable inspiration to millions. His writings and teachings have been studied for thousands of years and it seems very appropriate that on his birthday we should remind ourselves of at least a fragment of his indisputable wisdom, so if life feels as though it contains nothing but difficulties, remember that he reminds us:

In a world where we arrive to encounter gentleness, our task is then to press forward in order to overcome hardness.

Tuesday August 1 – The Metal Rabbit – Essence of the day is Wood

This is a good day to make progress: there is every indication of it being a very active day, so it is up to us to make the most of it. Weddings are favoured, because the Almanac informs us that these will result in rich and prosperous descendants. Since travel is also regarded as very auspicious, not only should the bride arrive on time, but if she and her groom leave for their honeymoon today, going with the flow should provide the icing on the cake, ensuring that they both have the perfect day. Since we are informed that it is a day when 'hidden treasure' may present itself, anyone going to an auction or a sale of any kind, or looking around for a bargain, should keep their eyes open extra wide as they could be lucky and find more than they ever hoped for.

What would be the point of dreams, if nobody's dreams came true?

Wednesday August 2 – The Water Dragon – Essence of the day is Water

Another day to feel optimistic and to promote yourself and your ideas in a positive way, because, without your effort, nothing can really take place, whereas a great deal can be achieved with your co-operation and encouragement. Study, education and self-cultivation are all advised today, so if you do have any homework, essays or lectures to prepare, go with the flow, sit down and attend to them today. These favourable influences affect not only the student but the teacher as well, so pay particular attention if you are attending a lecture or seminar today because if your teachers have done their homework, they are certain to be more eloquent, precise and illuminating than usual, even by their own high standards.

Thursday August 3 – The Water Snake – Essence of the day is Water

Another very auspicious day and if you are feeling a little tired, don't worry about it today, because tomorrow you will have the opportunity to take things easier when the energy is not as favourable. Not a day to squander, but a day to use your energy to good effect so that your progress can continue and your hopes and aspirations flourish. Networking would be a very productive way to spend the day, so check your e-mail, get on the telephone and start communicating with others, because Respected Master T'ung reminds us that for today at least, all avenues are open to us.

Friday August 4 – The Wood Horse – Essence of the day is Metal

As predicted yesterday, today is a very different kettle of fish and one with the lid firmly on, because this is the day when everything is said to be 'closed for business'. Today is very much a day of concealment, and one that was often chosen for burials, so it is also a day when it will pay to keep a low profile. The Constellation is the Ox Boy, weeping for his lover, the Weaving Maiden, and this adds a depressing edge to the day. To counteract that, the wise approach would be to keep in mind all the positive aspects of our lives and find a beneficial activity requiring will-power and determination. It would therefore be an excellent day to give up smoking, to begin a new diet or start some other new routine which, although difficult, will bring additional benefits to your life. Be positive and try to avoid behaving like the proverb that says:

 You are looking in front, but disregarding the rear.

Saturday August 5 – The Wood Sheep – Essence of the day is Metal

Today is a lot more inspiring and although it would not be wise to speculate with finances too much, there is much that can be done to enhance your future prospects. A very good day for those in business, because the influences favour trading of all kinds today, so try to go with the flow and join in the activity with enthusiasm. If you are stuck at home and the weather is good, try to avoid heavy manual work in the garden and find other jobs that are less physically demanding but equally important. Entertaining at home is fairly favourable, so if you feel like inviting a few friends over and having a bit of a party, the Almanac would certainly not raise any objections.

Sunday August 6 – The Fire Monkey – Essence of the day is Fire

Today is the seventh day of the seventh Moon and this is considered by many to be a very inauspicious day, since this month is often associated with the month of ghosts. There is one lovely aspect about today, however, which we should all try to keep in mind because it may encourage us all to treat our partners even better. Heaven has decided, in its mercy, to allow the Ox Boy and his lover, the Weaving Maiden, to meet today by crossing a bridge over the Milky Way made of millions of flying magpies. This event only takes place once a year, according to the terms of their separation imposed on them by Heaven for their failure to attend to their duties and for neglecting their tasks. It is a sad story which should serve as a reminder of how different our lives would be if we lost our partner for any reason, so it would be very appropriate to make a little extra effort today to let your partner know just how much you appreciate them.

Monday August 7 – The Fire Rooster – Essence of the day is Fire

Today marks the solar chi festival of Li Ch'iu, which marks the beginning of Autumn, the season associated with the harvest and the Metal element. This first month of Autumn is still very much influenced by the yang energy, because although it has been declining since the Summer solstice when it reached its peak, it is still the dominant force. It is a time when we should use our energy to harvest and gather wealth and resources to see us through the Winter. Respected Master T'ung reminds us that it would be wise to sweep away negative and disruptive influences today, so obviously feng shui remedies would be very favourable if you can make time to clear the decks and prepare for action.

Tuesday August 8 – The Earth Dog – Essence of the day is Wood

The business of the week can really get under way today because the energy favours activity of all kinds, so not a day to waste on trivial matters – the Almanac clearly favours things of importance. Obviously those in business can prosper today, especially if they are attending important functions or meetings, since the energy indicates a positive outcome for all concerned. Weddings and other social functions are also in a very good position to benefit from the favourable influences because not only do these events have the blessing of the Emperor himself, they also have the approval of Heaven. Moving into a new house, going on holiday and travel in general are all considered to be favourable, so there is no excuse – everyone can find something to do today.

Wednesday August 9 – The Earth Pig – Essence of the day is Wood

The favourable aspects of yesterday remain a positive influence, which should help enable everyone to continue where they left off without any disruption, so face the day with an enthusiastic attitude, because once again everything is in your favour. If the events of the last few days have focused around business, remember, now that we are in the season of Autumn, associated with the Metal element, this is the season of money and an excellent time to begin to harvest some of this for yourself. This is especially applicable to anything that was begun in the Spring and that you developed and encouraged during the Summer, so don't be surprised if your financial position takes a marked turn for the better.

Thursday August 10 – The Metal Rat – Essence of the day is Earth

Another day when it will pay everyone to keep busy, even if there are fewer opportunities than yesterday, because in order to keep the flow going, we need to make an effort every day. The daily influences favour those who go about their business quietly, because Respected Master T'ung warns everyone not to make any false accusations against others today. Failure to heed this advice will result in serious consequences. The smart approach would be to stay out of other people's business today and if there are issues that you need to raise, wait until a more appropriate time when the energy is more harmonious. If you needed further evidence, then consider the following:

 *A spark from a single fire can burn a million acres,
just as a single wrong expression can ruin
a lifetime's reputation.*

Friday August 11 – The Metal Ox – Essence of the day is Earth

An auspicious day really, which should provide those at work with the inspiration and energy to end this week on a prosperous note, so don't complain about having to go to work – put on your best smile and enjoy the prospect of a rewarding day. For those at home today, the influences favour those who keep themselves busy, and fortunately domestic activity is also regarded as very beneficial. Of course, this does place a responsibility on everyone to make use of their time in the most productive way, but at least if we do, we are likely to prosper, which isn't always the case. Try to avoid too much travelling and even if you have taken possession of the keys to your dream home, it would be prudent to select another day to move into it, because this is something that the Almanac advises against, for today at least.

Saturday August 12 – The Water Tiger – Essence of the day is Metal

A difficult day, and one which in China is considered by many to be a day when criminals are punished. Clearly that makes it a day that favours those in authority and puts the onus on them to behave accordingly and not to abuse their power. It is always difficult to deal with conflict and, even with the best training possible, it is still a very demanding task; so if we want those in authority to do a good job, we all have a responsibility to try to help them. We can only make matters worse by taking an aggressive stance: if either party uses that approach today, everyone will have cause for regret.

Sunday August 13 – The Water Rabbit – Essence of the day is Metal

Although there is less cause for concern than yesterday, don't expect too much from your efforts: things may not turn out the way you would like, so be prepared for a few surprises. If you are at home spending the day with the family, try to avoid raising controversial issues and view it as a day of celebration rather than an opportunity for retribution. A day to go with the flow, make it easy on yourself and you will make it easy on others. Consider the fact that if everyone took that attitude, there would be a lot more understanding and compassion available for those who really need it.

Monday August 14 – The Wood Dragon – Essence of the day is Fire

Today is not only the day of the Full Moon, but also the Chinese Festival of Hungry Ghosts. There are basically two types of hungry ghost. The first is the spirit of someone who either committed suicide or who died a premature and violent death and as a result is forced to wait out their allotted time here on Earth before they can proceed on their journey. The other type is someone who died without leaving any descendants to make the necessary provisions for them to pass into the next world. The only way for these spirits to alleviate their situation is to take over the body of a living person and today, according to legend, the gates of a thousand hells are opened and all the ghosts come rushing out. Candles are lit and offerings are made to them to appease their appetites, and in Hong Kong, huge operas are staged to amuse the ghosts while they feast on the offerings. It would be good feng shui to light a few candles to remember all those who have no one to care for them.

Tuesday August 15 – The Wood Snake – Essence of the day is Fire

A good opportunity to get the week off to a flying start, because business and trading in general are very well favoured. Not a day to miss out on then, but one in which it would be advisable to take an active role, if not the lead part, in what is going on. As always, it is up to us to utilise the positive energies as best we can. Outside activites are also considered to be very much in harmony today and if the weather is nice, that broadens the options still further. Since studying is also considered to be favourable, those who don't fancy doing any work in the garden could always sit outside and read a book, but remember the Chinese adage that tells us:

 A good man doing good finds the day is not long enough.

Wednesday August 16 – The Fire Horse – Essence of the day is Water

Another good day when you should try to tap into any positive energies, because once again the emphasis is on activity; so providing we make use of these favourable conditions, much can be accomplished today. Music and the arts in general are very well favoured and this also applies to anything that requires a creative input, so whether you are a designer, a window dresser or an actress, try to make good use of this heavenly inspiration. Respected Master T'ung also suggests that we use at least part of the day to contact friends, family and loved ones, so go on – make that connection.

Thursday August 17 – The Fire Sheep – Essence of the day is Water

The portents today suggest confusion more than anything else, so there is nothing too drastic to worry about, but be prepared to face a few minor obstacles. A day when it may be difficult to get into your flow, but if you overcome this minor setback, then you should still be able to make some progress. If you have already had an opportunity to harvest some of your wealth, then perhaps you should consider putting some to one side because today favours those who put something into their store cupboard. Autumn is the season of harvest, but as well as gathering in we should also store some away for the winter.

Friday August 18 – The Earth Monkey – Essence of the day is Earth

A peculiar day, partly because the Constellation is represented by the Ghostly Carriage – when the spirit world is active – although since this is not combined with anything harmful, it indicates a day when these influences can be utilised for beneficial aspects. If you enjoy astrology of any kind, or you like to have a tarot reading from time to time, today would be very suitable, because at least some of the influences have connections with the spirit world. Clairvoyants, psychics and those studying the paranormal are certain to receive more help than usual, and any form of meditation or personal cultivation would also benefit from being in harmony with the day.

 The way out into the light often looks dark.

Saturday August 19 – The Earth Rooster – Essence of the day is Earth

Sporting events are very much the flavour of the day, especially if you are participating, so whether you intend playing tennis, competing in an athletics event or just jogging in the park, you are very much in harmony today. Alternative therapies and remedies of all kinds are also appropriate, because matters relating to health are highlighted, so if you have been considering seeing your doctor or therapist, today would be a good time to do it. Feng shui remedies are obviously very suitable today and since it is the season of harvest, anything that is done to create more space will encourage even more prospects to come your way.

Sunday August 20 – The Metal Dog – Essence of the day is Metal

Mixed fortunes today really, but the emphasis is very much in favour of positive aspects so this should be kept in mind. It is not likely to be a good day for tackling mundane, routine tasks, because, as Respected Master T'ung reminds us, today is represented by the Chinese character Man, which means 'full' or 'complete'. A day, then, which favours matters of importance, irrespective of whether they are related to business or pleasure, and since it is Sunday, perhaps it would be a nice idea to treat the family to a day out. Travel is fairly favourable, so there is no excuse not to get out and about, and if you do decide to have some fun, then take it as seriously as you treat your work. No half-measures – make it a day to remember.

Monday August 21 – The Metal Pig – Essence of the day is Metal

If you have been waiting for a good day to move into your new house, you can proceed with confidence today, because everything indicates that today is a very appropriate time. If you are at work, don't hesitate, you can start as you mean to go on, this is not a day to shirk responsibility. If you are stuck at home for any reason, try to avoid doing any work in the garden, especially digging, although light duties such as watering should be fairly suitable. If the weather is nice, you may well be tempted just to sit outside and enjoy it, and if this is how you feel today, try to use the time productively and contemplate how you can use the rest of the week to your advantage.

Tuesday August 22 – The Water Rat – Essence of the day is Wood

Definitely a day which should be made use of, but not a day that favours the faint-hearted because the emphasis is on hard work. Laziness will not be tolerated today, so it is important to adopt a positive, enthusiastic approach to your duties, because nothing less than maximum effort will do. This applies whether you are at home, at work or even on holiday, so if you want to inspire those around you, or you want to get the most from your workforce, the best approach would be to lead by example. If you need any further evidence of the wisdom to this approach, consider the following Chinese proverb:

 When those in a superior position are dedicated to their cause, those below them will be even more devoted.

Wednesday August 23 – The Water Ox – Essence of the day is Wood

Today is the solar chi festival of Ch'u Shu, which means 'heat finishes', and this is nature's indication that we are in the last solar fortnight, influenced by the Summer Fire. The last gasp of Summer energy, then, which is something that we should all try to make use of, especially today when the daily influences encourage activity of all kinds. Weddings are again very well favoured, not only because the Emperor himself bestows his blessings, but also because the Almanac informs us that children born of a marriage today will become very gifted and that they will bring great honour to their parents. Everyone should try to keep themselves busy today, because if you apply yourself, you may be surprised just how much you can accomplish, and during this time of the year, whether you are at home or at work, there is always plenty to do.

Thursday August 24 – The Wood Tiger – Essence of the day is Water

A very peculiar day: the combinations could not be more contradictory. The best advice would be listen to everything going on around you but don't follow any of it, because otherwise you would be forced to take sides, which would not be a very wise thing to do. Definitely a day to vote for 'none of the above' and to remain independent, especially if you encounter any kind of hostility. It will pay to be careful today, to keep a low profile and to avoid getting side-tracked, because things are not what they appear, so keep in mind the following Chinese poem:

Across the river is an ingot of gold,
but the river is deep and wide
and that golden prize you will never hold,
because you are standing on the opposite side.

Friday August 25 – The Wood Rabbit – Essence of the day is Water

A massive improvement on yesterday: things are back in harmony, although not in a particularly favourable combination, so it would still be wise to exercise a little more caution than usual. It would be smart to dig out your sense of humour today, because this would be by far the best approach to the day. You may find that no matter what you do, there are certain aspects of your life that you don't seem to be able to make any impact on at all, and if that is the case, divert your attention to something that offers less resistance. Go with the flow today and if you like the idea of going out for a few drinks after work, that's okay, because the Almanac at least understands how you feel and as long as you are responsible, it may be just the tonic you need.

Saturday August 26 – The Fire Dragon – Essence of the day is Earth

Today provides the opportunity to get back on track, encouraging a much more positive approach to almost everything that is carried out. There's no time to lose, and if you have found the last few days difficult, put it all behind you and start again because your prospects have certainly improved. Travel is considered to be fairly favourable, so as there is no need to stay close to home, perhaps you should consider broadening your horizons and looking in other directions. If you are going on holiday, you can afford to have a big smile on your face because not only do you have the delicious expectation of a period of rest and rejuvenation to look forward to, but you have selected a very auspicious day to begin.

Sunday August 27 – The Fire Snake – Essence of the day is Earth

Another very active day and one that places an emphasis on the home, although not necessarily focusing on domestic duties. An excellent opportunity to get together with friends, family and loved ones, and since outside activities are also considered to be very auspicious, it should provide the motivation to tidy up the garden, soak up the remaining heat of the Summer and have a barbecue. Next week will bring a New Moon, which will add a fresh impetus of vitality to the proceedings, so perhaps it would be wise to use your energy to make time for some of the more pleasurable aspects of life, like family and loved ones.

Monday August 28 – The Earth Horse – Essence of the day is Fire

A fairly auspicious start to the week, although, with the New Moon tomorrow, today provides more of a launching pad for the week ahead rather than the actual lift-off. A day of preparation, then, which is every bit as important even if it is much less glamorous than putting the finishing touches to something and receiving all the credit. The whole process of harvesting consists of a lot of hard, back-breaking work and it is often the most demanding aspect in the annual cycle of production, but somebody has to do it and it would be wrong to expect others to do it for us. Look at it as the most enjoyable aspect of our duties, because after planting the seeds and spending all Summer nourishing and nurturing those hopes and dreams, Autumn provides us with the opportunity to turn them into reality. Learn to switch into nature's natural energy cycles and go with the flow and the quality of your life and experiences are likely to improve beyond measure.

Month 8

The New Moon for this month is, of course, the harvest Moon, the brightest and fullest of them all, so keep this in mind as a source of inspiration over the coming few weeks and remind yourself to make best use of it to encourage your own harvesting efforts. It is also wise always to remember that this is the time to begin to store resources so that we have some in reserve for the Winter, a time when we usually need them the most. Gathering and storing, then, are the orders for the month and the more effort that is put into this department, the less you will have to fear from the Winter. If you are enthusiastic in your approach, you can look forward to a time when you can rest and replenish yourself and nurture your vitality – but in the meantime there is work to be done, physically and metaphorically.

An active day that should promote industry and activity, so good news for those in business, because today favours trading and dealings of all kinds. Respected Master T'ung informs us that it would be very appropriate not only to chase up any outstanding accounts, but also to pay any bills that may be overdue. One encourages the other and all symbiotic relationships should be encouraged because this is what harmony is all about. Travel is also favoured and this will enable everyone to get around quickly and efficiently, so there are no excuses and it will benefit everyone to participate in the day's events.

Today is the birthday of Tsao Chun or Tsao Wang, who is known as the kitchen god and whose image is often placed on the wall of the kitchen at the New Year. He is a symbol of our connection with Heaven, because his role is to report our actions to the Jade Emperor, so it would be sensible not to forget his birthday and if you want to butter him up, light a few candles in his honour today. Appropriately, it is also the day of cleansing when we are encouraged to sweep away negative influences, so perhaps it would be wise to give the kitchen a good clean today in order to make the best possible impression. Feng shui remedies are obviously in the flow, so if you feel like doing some space-clearing, then today would seem the obvious choice.

Friday September 1 – The Water Dog – Essence of the day is Water

An encouraging end to the week for those in business because important meetings, functions and discussions of all kinds are considered to be very favourable today. If you were waiting for an opportunity to ask the boss for a rise, applying for a promotion within the company or attending a job interview, don't be hesitant, because everything points to a successful outcome today. With such favourable conditions, it would be silly to waste them on petty issues because this is a day to go for it – and the bigger, the better. Remember that the secret is making the most of your good luck and if you don't try to make the most from the favourable prospects today, then you only have yourself to blame. Seize the moment!

Saturday September 2 – The Water Pig – Essence of the day is Water

If you are in full flow at the moment, it is difficult to see how anything could be capable of putting you off, in which case it is a question of business as usual; but if matters are concluded, it would be a good idea to spend a little time contemplating the future. Often we realise too late that with a little more planning and forethought, we could have saved ourselves time and energy, not to mention money, and we have to put it down to experience. Only by looking at the whole picture can we really see the best approach and this can only be carried out by considering every aspect. As Lao Tzu teaches us:

 If you desire to breathe deeply, you must first empty the lungs: if you desire to be strong, you must first learn to be weak.

Sunday September 3 – The Wood Rat – Essence of the day is Metal

A fairly auspicious day, suitable for all kinds of activity, so whether you are at work, at home or on holiday, try to make the most of it. Outside activities are very favourable and if you have a garden and you find yourself at home, then perhaps you should consider focusing your attentions there, or you could look at some external DIY round the house. The weather will change shortly and before we know it, Winter will be upon us, so it is important to use the Autumn as much as we can to absorb the last part of the heat of the year. It is the perfect way to recharge our own personal batteries, providing energy, encouragement and enthusiasm – essential attributes which help us to go with the flow.

Monday September 4 – The Wood Ox – Essence of the day is Metal

Not the most encouraging start to the week, but it will get better, and if you can show some determination and willingness today, then the chances are that the influences will support rather than hinder you. If you are at home today, then you have an even bigger responsibility, because the influences indicate that domestic activity is very favourable; not the glamorous, entertaining type, but the more mundane, everyday matters. It would not be wise to tackle any difficult tasks, especially if you don't really know what you are doing or you don't have the right tools for the job, because you might get into more trouble than you bargained for, so keep in mind the Chinese proverb that tells us:

 Without weapons one does not attack a tiger, and without a boat one cannot cross a great river.

Tuesday September 5 – The Fire Tiger – Essence of the day is Fire

If you can avoid negative aspects today, then you should still be able to make progress, even though you may not think so. A demanding day in many respects, not least because if you are to survive unscathed, you may not only have to utilise all your powers of diplomacy, but also show considerable restraint. Conflict is in the air, but if you are aware of it, there is no reason why you should not be able to avoid it, and the best way to do that is to concentrate on the positive aspects of the day. Business can still prosper, and matters relating to the home are also very favourable, so if you don't expect too much from the day's events, you won't run the risk of being disappointed.

Wednesday September 6 – The Fire Rabbit – Essence of the day is Fire

Another day when it will pay to get on with your work without shouting about it too much; you cannot expect to be rewarded every day. The fact that you might not get paid today should not be used as an excuse to put in a half-hearted effort, because although others may not notice, the Jade Emperor will certainly be informed. That being the case, he will only make a deduction from your wages and he may not be as lenient as you would like, so do yourself a favour and eliminate the possibility by giving your full attention to whatever you do. If your motives are good and your attitude is commendable, who knows, you may even be rewarded for your efforts, but don't be too disappointed if this doesn't happen: it does not necessarily mean that your actions have gone unnoticed.

Thursday September 7 – The Earth Dragon – Essence of the day is Wood

Today marks the solar chi festival of Pai Lu, which means 'white dew', and as the name suggests, this is a time associated with the first frosts. This is the beginning of the second month of Autumn, when the Metal chi really begins to exert its influence, and it is nature's way of letting us know that the business of harvest must be taken seriously now as there is no more time to lose. This next solar fortnight will bring a change in the weather and it is very important to stress that this is the last period of the year when the Yang energy is the dominant force. After the Autumn equinox, the yin energy begins to take over, so it is important to use this coming active period as much as possible, because after this, things become more difficult.

Friday September 8 – The Earth Snake – Essence of the day is Wood

An excellent opportunity to end the week with a flourish because all the indications point to a successful outcome, so not a day to miss out on. Traditionally, during the time of harvest, many families all join in and work on a rota basis, combining their strength, knowledge and expertise to enable everyone to complete the harvest before the onslaught of Winter. If you prepared the ground in the previous Winter, planted extensively during the Spring, worked hard over the Summer and were also fortunate enough to receive nature's blessing, you could well have an extensive harvest. That being the case, you will need the help of others, so keep this in mind, because there are helpful people out there, but you do have to look for them or at least be aware that they are there, so keep in mind the Chinese proverb that says:

 When three men are of one heart, yellow earth is turned into gold.

Saturday September 9 – The Metal Horse – Essence of the day is Earth

Another very prosperous day that provides the perfect conditions for harvesting, so get the tractor out and hitch up the trailer – literally or metaphorically speaking! – because you never know, you may have a bumper crop. A good day for trading and business in general, but also a day when education receives an additional boost, so anyone needing to study should find it relatively easy, providing of course that they make an effort. Weddings are also particularly auspicious because the Almanac informs us that children born of a marriage contracted today will become friends of the Emperor himself, so clearly, with connections like that, they are sure to go far.

Sunday September 10 – The Metal Sheep – Essence of the day is Earth

Another fairly auspicious day, although one that favours less frantic activity, which is fairly appropriate for Sunday. A good day to relax, chill out and take it easy. Respected Master T'ung indicates that today is the official day of recuperation, because the Heavenly Doctor is on duty, so anyone who has been ill recently should benefit from his assistance. Music, arts and crafts and creativity of all kinds are favoured, so if you are looking for further inspiration, try to tune into the favourable influences that are readily available for everyone to harness.

Monday September 11 – The Water Monkey – Essence of the day is Metal

Not the most auspicious start to the week but it could be a lot worse, so if it takes you a little time to get into your stride, don't worry too much because it is only nature's way of providing us all with a few challenges to prevent us from taking too much for granted. The positive aspects of the day should encourage everyone to use their energy to seek out opportunities, because although these may be difficult to catch, the act of participation is very desirable today. We cannot expect to win every game we play, but if we don't participate, we don't have any chance, and only by playing regularly can we develop and sharpen our skills.

A wise workman always sharpens his tools before he commences work.

Tuesday September 12 – The Water Rooster – Essence of the day is Metal

Today marks the day of the Full Moon and this is considered to be the mid-Autumn festival, or Moon festival, because many consider it to be the birthday of the Moon. At this time of the year, around the Autumn equinox, the Moon often appears larger than usual, and if the night is clear it is certain to be a magnificent sight. The ancient Chinese often organised Moon-watching parties, a tradition which still continues today. As usual, special foods are prepared to mark the occasion and this is the day for eating the fabulous Moon cakes, sweet delicacies that are often sent to friends, families and loved ones. These are always exquisitely packaged, often quite expensive and there are numerous shops in Hong Kong and Taiwan that specialise in sending them to Chinese communities all over the world. The equinox is still more than a week away, so as you gaze at the Moon tonight, remember that the yin energy will soon become the dominant force, and remind yourself to make the most of the remaining yang chi and look to pulling in and storing up your reserves.

Wednesday September 13 – The Wood Dog – Essence of the day is Fire

Today is regarded as the birthday of the monkey king, or Sun Hou-tzu, to give him his correct title, the key figure in *The Journey to the West,* one of the best-known and most loved of all Chinese stories. It is like a Chinese version of *Pilgrim's Progress* and it records the tale of monkey and his small band travelling to the West to bring back sacred Buddhist scriptures for the Emperor; in effect, it dramatises the introduction of Buddhism into China and is full of ghosts, demons, fairies and magic spells. It would be very good feng shui to light some candles in the monkey king's honour today, and if there are obstacles or problems in your life that you would like some help with, ask for his support: his energy and willingness to help us knows no bounds.

Thursday September 14 – The Wood Pig – Essence of the day is Fire

An active day that will suit everyone with important issues on their agenda, today favours matters of significance. For those in business, there's an opportunity to secure contracts, finance, new markets and other opportunities that may present themselves, so it is important to be enthusiastic and confident, which helps to inspire the same in others. It is the perfect day to move into your new dream house, so if you have the keys, don't delay because travel, movement and activity in general are all very favourable. Try to avoid routine or petty tasks – leave those for another day when conditions are less favourable – and focus on more pressing issues.

Friday September 15 – The Fire Rat – Essence of the day is Water

The weekend is coming up and for many people this is the last day at work, which provides an opportunity to end on a balanced, orderly note. Don't leave your desk or workplace in a mess, because it will only have a negative effect when you return; so even if you don't want to disturb things too much, try to leave everything in an orderly fashion. If things are going a little slower than you had planned, it is important not to panic because Respected Master T'ung reminds us that this is the day of P'ing, which means 'balance', so it is important not to lose sight of that. If your plans, projects or aspirations are behind schedule, spend some time today contemplating how you can get them back on track, and take some encouragement from the fact that there is time left to achieve your aims and gather in your harvest before Winter begins. With the right attitude, a positive approach and a happy and enthusiastic outlook, much can be achieved, even if you have to start from rock-bottom.

Saturday September 16 – The Fire Ox – Essence of the day is Water

Another day to keep yourself busy and not to dwell on negative thoughts, especially if these are connected with the loss of a partner or loved one, because this reflects the negative aspects of the daily influences. The way forward is to bury yourself in a deluge of activity and it really doesn't matter if this is related to business, or pure, unadulterated pleasure. Leisure activities are very well favoured, so if you do have the opportunity to take the day off and enjoy yourself, you should try to make use of it. Balance is the key, and for this reason you should consider taking time out when you can because this all helps to refresh and rejuvenate you, ready for the next bout of activity, so take your leisure time more seriously because it is an important part of the flow of life.

Sunday September 17 – The Earth Tiger – Essence of the day is Earth

A very good day to stay close to home, and the influences very much favour a family day, when everyone has the opportunity to make a contribution towards a productive and rewarding day that will benefit the whole family. Domestic activity is considered to be necessary, but this is not confined to the inside because outside activities are also very favourable, so there should be something to suit everyone. For those who want to dash around, keep in mind the fact that Respected Master T'ung advises us against travel today, but if this cannot be avoided, then you should allow plenty of time for the journey, because you may well encounter congestion and delays.

Monday September 18 – The Earth Rabbit – Essence of the day is Earth

A day when the right hand doesn't seem to know where the left hand is, let alone what it is doing; confusion is everywhere. Conflict and opportunities appear to go hand in hand today, and the best advice for everyone would be to keep out of other people's affairs and focus on their own business. Not a day for face-to-face confrontation of any kind, because today there will be no winners, only losers, so unless you want to be a loser, avoid taking an aggressive attitude towards anything or anyone, even if you think it will have a positive effect. Keep both feet firmly on the ground today – it won't pay to take any chances.

He who stands on tiptoe is not steady,
and he who has stiff legs cannot walk easily.

Tuesday September 19 – The Metal Dragon – Essence of the day is Metal

An improvement on yesterday, so it should be a lot easier to go with the flow today, which should enable everyone to benefit. A day when everyone can prosper, although it will not pay to be too demanding because you might not have a say in matters, so just be content with whatever happens. Respected Master T'ung reminds us that there is no point in climbing up a mountain against the wind, so keep this in mind, go with the flow and try to enjoy yourself. The secret is to take a light-hearted approach to life's problems, dig out your best sense of humour and try to enjoy whatever the day brings.

Wednesday September 20 – The Metal Snake – Essence of the day is Metal

A very auspicious day that should encourage everyone to strive to maintain maximum effort because you can accomplish great things today. If you are at work or in business, try to be as energetic as possible, and since travel is also considered to be auspicious, there is every reason to broaden your horizons. Weddings are also very favourable, and relationships can benefit as well as commerce, so you should try to make the most of the positive energies. Outside activities are also very favourable, especially the construction of dragon terraces, a reference to feng shui-enhancing landscape garden design, which, the Almanac informs us, is particularly appropriate today.

Thursday September 21 – The Water Horse – Essence of the day is Wood

Another excellent day that favours activities of all kinds, including business, trading, marriage, investments, building and construction, so there is something for everyone. The weather doesn't really matter either because this applies whether you are indoors or out, so there are no excuses: everyone can benefit, providing of course that they make an effort. It is also the birthday of T'ao Yeh, a Chinese god associated with wealth and pleasure. If you feel like treating your partner tonight, then go the whole hog, because you have an opportunity to make it an unforgettable evening and, even more importantly, you have the means to do it.

Friday September 22 – The Water Sheep – Essence of the day is Wood

Another Friday, the end of the working week for many of us, and it would be wise to try to tie up all your loose ends today in order to make an assessment of your present situation. There is still plenty of the Autumn energy to come, but tomorrow is the Autumn equinox, marking another turning point in the year, and it would be wise to take this into account. The classical Chinese character for the word 'harvest' also means 'profit', because to the Chinese they are the same thing. They consider that you can only expect to profit from your own efforts and during the season of harvest, or profit, we should remind ourselves of this. By making an honest assessment of your situation, you provide yourself with an opportunity to spot any errors you may have made in your calculations, as the Chinese proverb implies:

> *A child but a foot-long requires at least three feet of cloth.*

Saturday September 23 – The Wood Monkey – Essence of the day is Water

Today is the solar chi festival of Ch'iu Fen, which relates to the Autumn equinox, and this marks a major change in nature's natural annual cycle because, like the Spring equinox, this is a time of year when day and night are of equal length, or as the Chinese think of it, when yin and yang are in perfect balance. From tomorrow, the nights become longer as the days get shorter, and to the Chinese this is when the yin energy begins to dominate as the yang energy goes into decline – the warning that Winter is approaching. It is also the middle day of Autumn, so try to make a concerted effort to use your time well as Autumn is the season of profit, full of Metal energy that can provide you with the will-power and determination to work towards your dreams.

Sunday September 24 – The Wood Rooster – Essence of the day is Water

Today is the birthday of K'ung Fu-tzu, more popularly known as Confucius, who has helped to shape all aspects of Chinese life, thought and culture over the last 2,000 years. He is probably known best for his thoughts and ideas which he wrote in a book of sayings, collectively known as the *Analects*. Confucianism, Taoism and Buddhism are known as the Three Doctrines, and while each of them differs from the others, they all share many fundamental concepts. Although feng shui was in use during the time of Confucius, it was still in its formative stage and very much the property of the Emperor, not for the use of ordinary people who were prohibited from practising it. However, it is something that was of concern to everyone and there is no doubt that many people consulted Confucius on this subject as it is mentioned in one of the *Analects*, in which he comments on how to select a good place to live:

> *When selecting a place of residence, one should always look for a place that has a good moral climate, because if not, how could one be called wise?*

Monday September 25 – The Fire Dog – Essence of the day is Earth

Perhaps it would be wise to follow the advice of Respected Master T'ung today and devote some time to health matters. If you have been considering visiting your doctor or therapist, then this would be a very favourable time to do it. Sporting activities of all kinds are also very favourable, so you have every excuse to visit the gym or the health spa after work in order to derive the maximum benefits possible from the influences of the day. Don't feel guilty, don't see it as self-indulgent, but look at it as 'going with the flow' and you will be surprised how refreshed and rejuvenated you will feel, enabling you to put even greater effort into your plans, schemes, hopes and dreams. Remember the Chinese proverb that says:

 We must be able to be at peace in order to be active in love.

Tuesday September 26 – The Fire Pig – Essence of the day is Earth

A very auspicious day that can inspire us all for the rest of the week; not a day to miss out on, but a day in which to participate. Large events of all kinds are very favourable, including weddings, moving house, meetings and conferences and with such favourable aspects for travel, there are no limits to what can be achieved today. Interviews are very favourable and this is good news for those seeking employment. Although this task is often depressing and unrewarding, try to lift yourself today because you only need to be lucky once. Today provides an opportunity to be in the right place at the right time and the best way to improve your chances of this happening to you is to get out and about and make use of this positive energy.

Wednesday September 27 – The Earth Rat – Essence of the day is Fire

With a New Moon tomorrow, it is very appropriate that Respected Master T'ung reminds us to balance ourselves today and to spend a little time contemplating our actions. If you have crystals hanging in your home or at work, it would be wise to clean them today to make them fresh and bright to enable them to absorb even more effectively the fresh, new energy of the New Moon tomorrow. Crystals are often used to 'bring rainbows into our lives' and if you want to enhance your rainbows, use the energies of today to clean and refresh your crystals.

Month 9

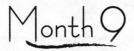

Thursday September 28 – The Earth Ox – Essence of the day is Fire

The New Moon today marks the beginning of the ninth lunar month and one that is considered by many to be associated with ghosts. The first nine days of this month are often used for fasting, in acknowledgement of the Nine Spirits of the North Star, and today is usually considered to be the day of preparation. Respected Master T'ung reminds everyone to keep busy today and this applies to those at home as well as those at work. So there are no excuses today; focus on your tasks and go about your work quietly and efficiently, and that way everyone can be left to benefit in their own way because it is the responsibility of everyone to prepare themselves. Keep in mind the Chinese proverb that warns us against following others:

 Beware of the blind man carrying a lantern; although the lamp lights his way, he still cannot see clearly.

Friday September 29 – The Metal Tiger – Essence of the day is Wood

Today favours those at home, not only because travel is considered something to be avoided, but also because the daily influences support domestic matters. For those of you working from home, today provides the perfect opportunity to spend the day catching up with anything that has been left for some reason and to rearrange your agenda if necessary. If you are left with a huge pile of housework to do, try not to be negative, go with the flow and think of how much happier you will feel when it is out of the way. If you feel like entertaining, tonight would be very appropriate, especially if you have been working hard all day, because then you will feel that you have deserved it.

Saturday September 30 – The Metal Rabbit – Essence of the day is Wood

If you have been thinking of having a party today, keep it to a small, intimate group – today is not really a good time for people to get together in large numbers. Conflict is the cause of the unfavourable aspects today and since prevention is often the best cure, perhaps the best course of action would be to keep a low profile. To avoid inviting trouble, it is often easier to stay away from it and in light of Respected Master T'ung's observations, crowds of people do not look very appealing, so keep in mind the Chinese proverb that tells us:

 When the nest falls, the eggs break.

FENG SHUI ALMANAC 2OOO

Sunday October 1 – The Water Dragon – Essence of the day is Water

A day to go with the flow; if you find yourself busy and enjoying it, then carry on, otherwise chill out, relax and put your feet up. Respected Master T'ung reminds us to be joyous today and since it is Sunday, perhaps it would be a good opportunity to have a day out somewhere either alone or with your partner, friends or family. This may provide the boost necessary to launch you into the coming week on a positive, enthusiastic note that will enable you to meet the challenges with a fresh approach. This is still the season of harvest and it is important to keep this in mind, because our actions now will determine our circumstances during the winter.

Monday October 2 – The Water Snake – Essence of the day is Water

An auspicious day in many respects, certainly if you are in business, because the portents favour an active day, but there is no reason why everyone should not benefit. Travel is very favourable and the further you venture, the better, especially if this involves staying away from home for any length of time. Business trips are obviously very favourable, so if you are in this position but you are saddened at the thought of being away from home, look on the bright side and consider the benefits that success will bring. If you are at home, outside activities are also considered to be fortunate, so if you have a garden and the weather is reasonable, it would be a good idea to spend some time attending to any jobs that need doing outside.

Tuesday October 3 – The Wood Horse – Essence of the day is Metal

Business and trading in general are considered to be very favourable today, so much so that we are even informed that it would be appropriate to 'open the treasuries', an indication that investments are considered to be good news today. However, this should not be used as an excuse to be reckless, but as an opportunity to improve your financial position and it is all part of the natural process of Autumn. Keep in mind the fact that this is the period to gather in your resources and to reap the benefits from your efforts, and this often means using further resources to carry this out effectively. We use the expression 'Speculate to accumulate', another good example of how the principles of yin and yang work on a day-to-day level, but it is important to remember that balance is the key, so don't overdo it.

Wednesday October 4 – The Wood Sheep – Essence of the day is Metal

Another auspicious day that favours an enthusiastic, positive approach, so try to make use of these favourable conditions to your best advantage by being active and alert. Respected Master T'ung suggests that we spend some time, at least, writing letters and getting in touch with others. Clearly it is a day to use your networking skills, so pick up the telephone, check your e-mail and start communicating. Music and the arts are also considered to be in harmony today and anyone looking for that extra little spark of creativity should not be disappointed, providing of course, that they make an effort to harness these favourable conditions.

Thursday October 5 – The Fire Monkey – Essence of the day is Fire

It may be difficult for today to flow smoothly, especially if you are working to a tight schedule, because things may not go the way that you would like them to. Everything points to the fact that obstacles may well present themselves, but mainly in the form of things being unavailable, as opposed to confrontational. If this is kept in mind and you resist the temptation to expect too much of a reward for your efforts, there is no reason why you should not be able to have a fairly productive day. Mind you, you may not be able to see the benefits for a while, but then that is often the case, so don't expect instant results and you may well be pleasantly surprised. Bear in mind the Chinese proverb that says:

   Fish cannot swim safely in shallow waters.

Friday October 6 – The Fire Rooster – Essence of the day is Fire

All the indications point to a very hectic end to the week: today favours activity of all kinds and whether you are at home or at work, you should try to make full use of this positive aspect to the day. Buying, selling, travelling and chasing up new opportunities are all considered to be in the flow today, so there is something to suit everyone. Today is also the Chinese festival of Chung Yang, which means 'climbing the heights', and this traditionally marks the start of the kite-flying season. Many people today walk up to the top of a high hill to acknowledge the occasion and this is definitely a day when all our hopes, dreams and aspirations can soar to new heights.

Saturday October 7 – The Earth Dog – Essence of the day is Wood

Sporting activities are very well favoured today, even more so if you are participating, but even as a spectator you are still making an important contribution to the events of the day. So if you feel like going to see a game of football or you would prefer a game of squash at your local sports centre, it is not necessary to try to find an excuse, just go and do it. Health matters are also highlighted today, so if you were planning a visit to your doctor or therapist, then today would seem to be a very appropriate time to do it. Don't delay, go with the flow and make use of the daily influences. The Chinese proverb reminds us:

 When a fault is known it should be amended, otherwise there is no reason for it to reveal itself.

Sunday October 8 – The Earth Pig – Essence of the day is Wood

Today is the solar chi festival of Han Lu, which means 'cold dew', and this marks the beginning of the last month of Autumn, so keep this in mind because this is an indication to look around and see what else is there for you to harvest. Feng shui remedies are also very well favoured, as Respected Master T'ung reminds us, so if you feel like enhancing your life using this ancient Chinese art, today would be a good day to begin activating your home. The best way to start would be to clear away any clutter that may be blocking the entrance or hallway and to have a good look around to see what needs repairing or replacing. It's no good trying to activate your wealth area by hanging wind chimes or other feng shui remedies if the wallpaper is hanging off the wall or the windows are cracked or dirty.

Monday October 9 – The Metal Rat – Essence of the day is Earth

An excellent start to the week and one that should encourage everyone to get off to a flying start because today has success written all over it. Important events of all kinds are considered to be very favourable, so whether you are giving a presentation or attending an important meeting, the influences will be working in your favour. Weddings are also particularly auspicious because the Almanac informs us that children born of a marriage conducted today will live a long life, which is what we all desire for our children.

 It is not important at what age one's children are born; what is important is that fate ensures they have a long life.

Tuesday October 10 – The Metal Ox – Essence of the day is Earth

For those of you in the flow, it is business as usual and you should continue where you left off yesterday, because today nature provides us with an extension, encouraging everyone to continue their efforts. If you had planned to move into a new home and for some reason this was not possible yesterday, today is also considered to be very favourable, so don't miss out on this golden opportunity to start your new life on a bright, auspicious note. If all your tasks have been accomplished, then spend a little time considering your position and look for ways to improve your harvesting abilities, because Winter will soon be upon us.

Wednesday October 11 – The Water Tiger – Essence of the day is Metal

Another very busy day that will suit all those who keep themselves occupied, irrespective of whether they are at home or at work: the key word today is activity. Building, construction, landscaping and agriculture are all favoured, in fact today almost anything goes, so there are no excuses and there is no point in kicking up a fuss if you don't want to participate, because that is just not an option. The smart thing to do is to use your energy to motivate yourself to begin, rather than waste it trying to justify not making a start, because for today at least, you will find yourself isolated if you adopt this attitude. However strong you think you are, the natural influences are stronger, so move with them and use their strength.

 The mighty Dragon is no match for the native Serpent.

Thursday October 12 – The Water Rabbit – Essence of the day is Metal

Travel is not considered to be very auspicious today, so try to avoid too much of this if possible; if not, allow plenty of time for your journey as you could be delayed. Matters relating to the home are considered to be in harmony today and Respected Master T'ung reminds us that domestic duties should be attended to, so if you are stuck at home for any reason, try to be productive, because that way something can be achieved. We are also advised to watch what we spend, so it is not a good day to go shopping. If you do, leave most of your credit cards at home as a precaution, because any reckless, impulsive shopping today will only give cause for regret.

Friday October 13 – The Wood Dragon – Essence of the day is Fire

For many here in the West, Friday the thirteenth does not have the best of reputations, and on this occasion, Respected Master T'ung is in full agreement, so treat these inauspicious omens with respect. Tread carefully today and stay alert, because it is important to avoid any negativity that would not only disrupt your flow, but may also escalate into something much worse. It is always better to be aware of the influences around us. There is nothing to be gained by contributing to the negative forces today and the most positive thing that you can do is to encourage others to follow your cautious example. As the Chinese remind us:

> *Frozen bean curd cannot be cut.*

Saturday October 14 – The Wood Snake – Essence of the day is Fire

There is no doubt that today is an improvement on yesterday, although it would be wise to start off slowly and not expect too much, because some of the negative aspects will still be lingering around. Not a day to force issues of any kind, so go with the flow and if you find yourself doing something that is not working very well, do something else that is easier. This is the perfect day to do what feels right and works, and if you can do this, you will be surprised just how much you achieve, so do whatever you feel like because it is not a matter of being selfish, to the Chinese, it is merely being sensible.

Sunday October 15 – The Fire Horse – Essence of the day is Water

An auspicious day in many respects, although some people may find it a little too hectic, especially if they had planned to have a day off, because today favours activity of all kinds. This applies not only to business and commerce but also to travel and movement in general, so whether you spend all day travelling, digging the garden or doing some DIY, you can be happy in the knowledge that you are going with the flow. The Autumn Earth season will be here soon and this will give everyone the opportunity to take a little time out, but in the meantime it would be wise to stay active and make full use of the active Autumn chi.

Monday October 16 – The Fire Sheep – Essence of the day is Water

The perfect start to the week and a day that should encourage everyone to leap into action, so start the day with a positive, enthusiastic attitude and grasp this opportunity with both hands. For those in business, the Almanac reminds us that this is the day for trading, so whether you are buying or selling, today has the opportunity to be very lucrative, even if that means indulging in a little speculation. Academic matters and study in general are also considered to be very favourable, as are meditation and personal cultivation, attributes that we all need to encourage in order to flow smoothly and therefore be at our most productive. The Chinese remind us of this in the proverb that says:

 Virtue is the root, wealth is the result.

Tuesday October 17 – The Earth Monkey – Essence of the day is Earth

Another fairly prosperous day, although not in the same league as the combined influences of yesterday, but that would be too much to expect. Although that sounds a little gloomy, look on the bright side: after all, there is only so much activity we can handle at any one time. Sometimes it only takes one opportunity to change our entire life, but when this appears, it is often due to an accumulation of events, some of which may have taken place years ago and which we may have forgotten. Recognising the sequences and cycles in your own life helps you to take a much more balanced view of current events, and looking back at where you may have gone wrong in the past should help you to avoid making those mistakes again, enabling you to enjoy your biggest harvest yet.

Wednesday October 18 – The Earth Rooster – Essence of the day is Earth

Today presents an odd mixture of elements, because on the one hand we are tempted by promises of good fortune in whatever we do, but on the other hand we are informed by Respected Master T'ung that everything is closed today. This suggests that the best course of action is window shopping and it would be very wise to regard any opportunities that may present themselves today in that light, because otherwise you may be very disappointed. If you have been feeling below par recently, try to take encouragement from the fact that the Heavenly Doctor is on duty today and as a result, your recuperation can now proceed, guided of course by his phenomenal expertise.

Thursday October 19 – The Metal Dog – Essence of the day is Metal

Today provides the perfect opportunity for a fresh start – both the Constellation and Respected Master T'ung indicate that this is the perfect day for new beginnings, ventures and projects of all kind. Of course, we are not in Spring, so this should be kept in mind, but this is the last day of the Metal period of Autumn. Tomorrow the Earth season begins and this means that today represents the last opportunity to make use of the active energy to prepare ourselves for the onslaught of Winter. The seasonal markers are nature's indicators, designed to make us aware of the changing climate and, as a result, to prepare ourselves accordingly. The Chinese treat the seasons with the greatest respect and they have no difficulty accepting that they determine the natural cycle of behaviour.

Cold comes, heat goes; gather in Autumn and store in Winter.

Friday October 20 – The Metal Pig – Essence of the day is Metal

Today is the first day of the Autumn Earth season and it is very appropriate that we are advised to sweep away negative influences, because this is the time when we can balance and adjust ourselves, ready to face the next phase of the annual cycle. The fewer obstacles we have, the easier it will be to achieve this, so a good clear-out of unwanted, stagnant, negative energy would be an excellent way to start. Feng shui remedies are obviously very well favoured, especially those designed to bring balance and harmony into our lives, as opposed to stimulating or activating specific areas. This is the last period of Autumn and it is vital that we continue to focus on our hopes, dreams and aspirations, because there is a lot of work to be done before we can enjoy the benefits of the Winter period.

Saturday October 21 – The Water Rat – Essence of the day is Wood

Another day of mixed fortunes really, but in general the emphasis is on positive actions, so if you keep that in mind you shouldn't go too far wrong. If you have important things to do today, especially regarding business, it would be wise to get them out of the way, because in many respects the daily influences encourage this. If you are travelling any distance, be prepared for delays, because although Respected Master T'ung informs us that the path is clear, the Constellation of the day is not in agreement, so it would be best to take precautions and that way you should not get caught out.

Sunday October 22 – The Water Ox – Essence of the day is Wood

An ideal opportunity presents itself today for those fortunate enough to have the day off; this is definitely a day to put your feet up, relax and chill out. There will be plenty of activity coming up next week but during the Earth season it is important to take some time to reflect and to ensure that we are still on course; there is no better time to do that than today, the day of P'ing, meaning 'balance'. The emphasis is very much on the home as far as the Constellation is concerned and this suggests that staying at home with the family and enjoying the positive aspects of domestic bliss would be the best course of action, so go with the flow and enjoy yourself.

Monday October 23 – The Wood Tiger – Essence of the day is Water

Today marks the solar chi festival of Shuang Chiang, which translates as 'frost descends' and this heralds the last solar fortnight of Autumn, another reminder that Winter is fast approaching. It is important at this time of the year not to get into Winter mode, however, even if the weather has wintry connotations, because there is still work to be done before the Autumn finishes. Try to keep busy today, because it is important that the coming week gets off to a good start and this applies equally to those at home and those at work, so there are no excuses. If you make an effort, you will prosper; it is as simple as that.

Tuesday October 24 – The Wood Rabbit – Essence of the day is Water

Another fortunate day, especially if you are lucky enough to be getting married, because the Almanac informs us that your descendants will be very rich. With a wedding present such as that, you can afford to walk down the aisle with a smile on your face – after all the Emperor doesn't send such heavenly gifts to every wedding. If for any reason you are stuck at home today, don't worry, because Heaven is also smiling on you and if you comply with the instruction that domestic matters should also be considered to be very important, then fortunate blessings are certain to come your way soon, even if they don't arrive today. It is always good to keep in mind the Chinese proverb:

 He who knows that he has enough is rich.

FENG SHUI ALMANAC 2000

Wednesday October 25 – The Fire Dragon – Essence of the day is Earth

A day to avoid any kind of conflict because, unfortunately, this is where the emphasis seems to be today; if you can do this, then there is no reason why today should not be profitable. A day to keep yourself to yourself because prevention is always better than cure, so don't invite trouble by involving yourself in the affairs of others. If you do become the target of abuse from others, don't let it upset you or prompt you to behave in a similar fashion, because for today, at least, it will pay to offer the other cheek. If you doubt the wisdom of this advice, consider the Chinese proverb:

 He who is unwilling to suffer trouble will never attain to being a man above other men.

Thursday October 26 – The Fire Snake – Essence of the day is Earth

Another day when it will pay to go with the flow, because anything else would be foolish. Let events dictate to you rather than you dictating the events. It is difficult to say what the most favourable activities are other than to say you should do whatever works best for you, because unless you try, you won't know. Go with your instincts today. With the New Moon arriving tomorrow, it would be wise to clean any crystals you may have hanging in the house and generally prepare for the fresh, new burst of energy that always arrives with a New Moon. This is a good day to reflect on your position and, since we are in the Earth season, a good time to try to see what adjustments and changes you could introduce to enable more beneficial influences to enter your life.

Month 10

Today's New Moon marks the beginning of the tenth lunar month according to the Chinese calendar and it would be wise to try to use this fresh burst of energy to get as much done as possible. The coming week is very important because it represents the last period of Autumn and it would be wise to gather as many benefits as possible before the time comes when we need to store and preserve our resources. Financial matters should be looked at very closely, because it would be better to start the Winter period with this aspect under control, so keep this in mind over the coming week. The objective, of course, is to try to make Winter as comfortable as possible, because this is the time when we replenish and nurture ourselves, when we eat and sleep more. The better the resources at our disposal, the more productive this period will be and the more benefits we can derive from it, so it is very important to make full use of the gathering period during the Autumn.

Today is fairly active, which should support those who keep themselves busy and apply their energy in a productive way. For those in business, the Almanac informs us that it is a good day for trading, so whether you are buying or selling, stay alert, because there will certainly be some lucrative opportunities. Travel is not considered to be very appropriate, so if you do have to make a journey, allow plenty of time or, better still, try to stay close to home. Students of all kinds are looked upon with particular favour today, especially if they devote their time to study, because this is something else which is very much in harmony with the day.

It is very appropriate that today is Sunday, because it is considered by many to be the beginning of the energy renewal cycle. A day of rest and recuperation really, emphasised by the fact that the Heavenly Doctor is once again on duty, which is good news for those who have been suffering with an illness. Music and the arts are considered to be very favourable today and it would be very appropriate to go to a concert tonight, visit an exhibition or go to the movies with a friend, because, with the added inspiration of the daily influences, it may well prove to be a memorable occasion.

Monday October 30 – The Metal Rooster – Essence of the day is Wood

Not the most auspicious start to week, so don't take anything for granted today, but on the other hand don't dwell on negative aspects. Perhaps the smart approach would be to use today as a preparation period for the coming week, because if nothing else, you can take this opportunity to look at your agenda and see if you can plan your week more effectively. Whether you are at home or at work, try to settle into a routine as quickly as possible because that way you are much more likely to be unaffected by the negative implications of the daily influences. As the Chinese say:

     A fallen tree casts no shade.

Tuesday October 31 – The Water Dog – Essence of the day is Water

The week can really get under way now because the influences encourage a day of activity. Everyone should treat this as a green light as you can really get ahead. Not a day to hesitate but a day to be confident, and the quicker you make a start, the more you can achieve. First impressions count, and it is important that we all try to look our best today, because with so much activity, it is impossible to know whom we may meet. The best course of action is to be prepared: if you're looking good, you're feeling good, and if you're feeling good, you perform better. Make an extra effort today because although success is fairly certain, your input and extra effort may make the difference between silver and gold.

Wednesday November 1 – The Water Pig – Essence of the day is Water

Another fairly auspicious day, especially if you intend to implement feng shui remedies to remove any obstacles to your progress as these will be particularly effective if they are carried out today. Travel is not considered to be very appropriate but sporting activities of all kinds are very favourably viewed, so if you had planned a visit to the gym after work, you could not select a more beneficial time. Health matters are also important, so a visit to the doctor or therapist would also be very much in the flow, and if this is something that you have been considering recently, don't delay any further.

Thursday November 2 – The Wood Rat – Essence of the day is Metal

A day that favours important events of all kinds, including meetings, conventions, functions and conferences, which all prosper today with the support of conditions favourable to success. Everyone should try to make use of this opportunity, so this is not a day to tackle routine, mundane issues, but a day to put your best foot forward and go where no one has gone before! If you are attending a job interview, extra effort will really be rewarded, so try to look your best and remember that first impressions go a long way. It may be frustrating at times to think that sometimes we are judged by how we appear rather than what we do, but remember that the other person has to make swift value-judgements in an interview situation, and they will assume that your smart and enthusiastic appearance will suggest that you have similar qualities in your personality.

 When a man is far from home, he is judged by
what he wears; when he is near to home,
he is judged by what he is.

Friday November 3 – The Wood Ox – Essence of the day is Metal

Everyone has the opportunity to finish the week with a flourish, because once again the portents are favourable, encouraging an active, positive attitude to the day. For those at work, today provides the opportunity to get up to date with any paperwork or accounts or anything else that needs doing, which may have been put off for some reason. It is always good to begin a new week with a fresh start and if you apply yourself today, you can achieve this over the next week and subsequently be in a better position to begin the Winter period. So make use of the last period of Autumn: Winter will soon be here.

Saturday November 4 – The Fire Tiger – Essence of the day is Fire

Another very auspicious day, especially for those getting married, for it is said that children born of a marriage conducted today will become very good friends of the Emperor, making their prospects for influential friends and supporters very bright. Outside activities are also favourable, so if you are at home and there are any jobs to do outside the house, today would be a very good day to attend to them. The important thing to remember is to avoid making any accusations; Respected Master T'ung warns of dire consequences for those who ignore this advice.

135

FENG SHUI ALMANAC 2OOO

Sunday November 5 – The Fire Rabbit – Essence of the day is Fire

Not a particularly good day to travel; it would be much wiser to stay near to home and avoid any complications that may arise. Domestic activity is considered to be very favourable today but that does not exclude socialising, so there is no reason why you shouldn't invite a few friends over and have a celebration, something which many people here in the UK will do since it is Guy Fawkes' night. With the essence of the day also associated with the Fire element, there is an increased risk of accidents tonight and since many families will be gathering around bonfires, an extra degree of caution will be needed, especially where children and animals are concerned.

Monday November 6 – The Earth Dragon – Essence of the day is Wood

Unfortunately, today does not represent the most auspicious start to the week, but nature doesn't always smile on us and the responsibility falls to us to make the most we can – even out of days like today. Determination can work wonders at times like these, but it is something that we have to instigate ourselves because nature cannot always help us. With the right approach and a positive attitude, something of benefit can always be achieved even in the face of conflict, and if this sounds simplistic, consider the Chinese proverb that tells us:

 It is easy to look at difficult work but it can be very difficult to carry it out.

Tuesday November 7 – The Earth Snake – Essence of the day is Wood

Today is the solar chi festival of Li Tung, which marks the beginning of Winter, associated with the Water element. This is the period of the year when plants, animals and yang energy in general are in decline and some go into hibernation. In an ideal world perhaps we would also hibernate during this period, but even though the idea may be appealing at times, it isn't especially practical! For us, it is business as usual – come wind, rain or snow – and this means that we have to try even harder to make an effort to nurture our vitality during this period. It is a time when we should all try to eat and sleep more, because during this part of the annual cycle we need to replenish and nurture ourselves in order to be ready again for the coming of Spring.

If a man does not store up vital forces in the Winter, he will be certain to suffer from an epidemic in the Spring.

Wednesday November 8 – The Metal Horse – Essence of the day is Earth

Not a day to make great headway, so don't expect too much in return for your efforts, although that's not an excuse not to try! Today is a day when it pays to go with the flow, and the secret is to get into a routine as quickly as possible. Try to choose something simple which presents no difficulties, because if there are any obstacles, the Almanac indicates that they are likely to be insurmountable, at least for today; so don't waste your energy on uphill tasks. With the coming of Winter, there will be a noticeable change in the climate over the next month and it is important to keep in mind the need to nourish ourselves and to balance the cold, wet, yin weather by keeping warm and dry. We also need to remember that the Winter period is a time to conserve and nurture our vitality and this cannot be stressed enough, because if we fail to do this and we start next Spring in a poor state, our chances of success are diminished drastically.

Thursday November 9 – The Metal Sheep – Essence of the day is Earth

An active day that should encourage everyone to go about their business; if you need to travel, then at least you should not encounter any difficulties. Outside activities are also considered to be very favourable and if there are any jobs that need doing and the weather is fairly reasonable, it would be very wise to make use of this opportunity. The concept of going with the flow is to avoid putting off for another day things that could be achieved today. If you always make use of the opportunities available, you will eventually balance your activities and get up to date, irrespective of how far you are behind to begin with. Like anything worthwhile this takes time, so don't expect immediate results although you will find that there are many benefits along the way.

Friday November 10 – The Water Monkey – Essence of the day is Metal

Today is the day of the Full Moon, so emotions may be running a little higher than usual, especially since the Water element is strengthened further by the influence of Metal, the essence of the day. Balance, as always, is the key and if we are faced with an emotional situation, it would be better for all concerned if we tried to remain as detached as possible, instead of reacting in a negative, aggressive way. A few kind words would be much more effective in calming the situation. We all need some encouragement and support from time to time and if we are feeling low, our need is even greater. In feng shui terms, people often ask me how they can encourage helpful people to come into their lives. As far as I am concerned, the most effective way to do this is to become a helpful person; if you are not prepared to help, you cannot expect others to help you.

Saturday November 11 – The Water Rooster – Essence of the day is Metal

Today is the birthday of the goddess Wu-shan, a deity who is associated with married couples, and it would be very good to acknowledge this today if you are married or in a long-term relationship. Traditionally, this is a day when people light candles, visit temples and give thanks for the life that they share with their partners and it would be good feng shui to follow this example. We often take our loved ones for granted and today provides us all with an opportunity to demonstrate just how much our partners and spouses mean to us. Dinner for two, candles, champagne, chocolates and the most important ingredient, loving, tender words, can all help to provide the perfect setting for a very memorable and exciting evening.

Sunday November 12 – The Wood Dog – Essence of the day is Fire

A day of mixed blessings really and not one to build your hopes on, because although many opportunities may appear to be tantalisingly close, Respected Master T'ung informs us that nature is closed for business today. An excellent opportunity to catch up with correspondence, so check your e-mail and get out your address book, because today favours contacting friends, family and loved ones. If you had planned to stay at home and do nothing, then there is nothing to prevent you from doing so, even if others don't support your actions. If this is the case, then point out that sometimes going with the flow means doing nothing.

 A wise traveller knows when it is time to travel and when it is time to rest.

Monday November 13 – The Wood Pig – Essence of the day is Fire

Today provides a very good opportunity to get the week off to a flying start, so however bad the weather looks from the bedroom window, try to look on the bright side as the daily influences will support positive actions which should provide some warmth and comfort. The best start would be to treat yourself to a really nourishing breakfast, collect your thoughts and focus on your likeliest chances of success. Trading and business in general are both very well favoured today but if you are stuck at home for any reason, try to keep busy as this too can bring profit. Although this requires a certain amount of effort, it is nowhere near what would be needed if the influences were against you, so if you consider this, today should be easy.

Tuesday November 14 – The Fire Rat – Essence of the day is Water

Feng shui remedies are considered to be very favourable today, because we are advised to sweep away all negative influences and obstacles. Health matters are also highlighted, so it would be a good idea to give this matter some consideration, especially if you have been neglecting yourself recently. Sporting activities are very much in harmony with the day, so perhaps you should consider visiting a gym or a sports centre. You are bound to feel better for doing this and may well want to make it a more regular part of your routine, which can only be to your benefit. In conjunction with proper nourishment and rest, this is just what the doctor ordered and if, like many, you like the idea but don't feel that you are up to it, today is an excellent opportunity to give it a go. Remember the Chinese proverb:

 A journey of a thousand miles begins with the first step.

Wednesday November 15 – The Fire Ox – Essence of the day is Water

An auspicious day that favours important and prestigious events; all the portents indicate that today is one of success. Weddings are obviously very favourable, but gatherings of all kinds will benefit from the positive influences of the day, so whether you are hosting a convention or attending an interview for a job, you can be confident that the force will be with you. Of course, on such an auspicious day there is every reason to look your best, so before you leave home to face the world and play your part in destiny, pamper yourself thoroughly to provide that additional feel-good factor.

Thursday November 16 – The Earth Tiger – Essence of the day is Earth

Another day to use to your advantage: once again the indications look very favourable, so stay active, keep alert and apply yourself accordingly. If you are still in the flow of yesterday, then you don't really have too much to think about, but if that business is concluded and you find yourself at a loose end, then there is no better time to sit back and reflect. Outside activities are not considered particularly auspicious, so if you are stuck at home and you feel like working around the house, try to avoid any heavy, manual work outside, because you will be better off leaving those jobs for another day.

Friday November 17 – The Earth Rabbit – Essence of the day is Earth

Another active day to be used to full effect, although it is perhaps not as auspicious as yesterday. Activity of all kinds is indicated, so what you do is not really important, because the emphasis is on the fact that you keep yourself busy and that you stay out of the affairs of others. It will pay dividends to go quietly about your business, keeping a low profile, because this is not a day to advertise or promote yourself. What matters is that you get things done, irrespective of whether or not you get the credit for it.

Saturday November 18 – The Metal Dragon – Essence of the day is Metal

It would be wise to stay close to home today; travel is not considered to be very suitable so this should be avoided if possible. Those who are at home today shouldn't worry too much, because they have the best deal in town; according to the Almanac, home is where the action is. If you work from home, then you should try to keep yourself busy because the inspiration is there for you to tap into. Once your work has been completed, the way is clear for some weekend entertaining.

Sunday November 19 – The Metal Snake – Essence of the day is Metal

The energy is very much in conflict today and it may be difficult to steer clear of these negative influences, in which case the best course of action is to prepare yourself. The positive aspects focus on matters relating to the home, which is very appropriate for a Sunday, and it would be wise to try to utilise this safe haven today. A good opportunity, to spend some time at home with the family and if you can adopt a light-hearted approach to any domestic disputes, the chances are that it will not spoil the day's events. However, it is important to stress that the onus is on everyone to pull together and make sure the atmosphere remains as positive as possible.

 When the water fails, the fish fly.

Monday November 20 – The Water Horse – Essence of the day is Wood

If you have an agenda or a schedule planned out today, that's fine, but don't be too rigid – be prepared to tear it up if events take off of their own accord. If you find yourself in this position, don't panic: it has nothing to do with you, it is only nature's way of reminding us that we should not take too much for granted. Respected Master T'ung reminds us to be happy, indicating that we should try to enjoy whatever we do, and if that is an excuse to pick and choose how we spend our time, it is an acceptable one, even if we allow events to dictate to us rather than the other way round. As the Chinese proverb tells us:

 The stones determine the flow of the stream.

Tuesday November 21 – The Water Sheep – Essence of the day is Wood

There are no excuses today and those at work can really get into their stride, because the influences favour activity of all kinds. Travel is also considered to be very favourable, so there is every opportunity to get out and about without the usual complications of delays and congestion. That should be encouraging news for anyone who needs to attend a meeting or interview, but if you are not at work, why not tap into these favourable conditions by visiting a friend or relative? The Almanac is giving you the green light to travel and you can make the most of it now.

Wednesday November 22 – The Wood Monkey – Essence of the day is Water

Today marks the solar chi festival of Hsiao Hsueh, which translates as 'little snow'. As the name suggests, it represents a point in time when Winter begins to take shape, with the emphasis focusing on the Water element. The portents suggest a day of trading, so everyone in business should try to exploit this aspect, even if this entails a certain amount of speculation. If you are a confirmed shopaholic, then it would be wise to find something else to do today – or at at least leave the credit cards at home, because today strongly favours the shopkeeper.

Thursday November 23 – The Wood Rooster – Essence of the day is Water

Today represents an even better proposition than yesterday, so there is every reason to feel optimistic about your prospects, however high your expectations may be. Reach for the stars and you may be surprised just how much you can accomplish, because for today everything appears to be available. Music lovers would be well advised to see what's on offer tonight because with such favourable influences, any public performances will certainly be even more inspiring than usual. This also applies to art exhibitions and theatrical productions, so if this appeals to you, treat yourself to an evening out. If you are going out, remember to make an effort to look your best, because you never know who you may bump into and as the Chinese proverb reminds us:

 Men honour the rich; even dogs bite those with ragged clothes.

Friday November 24 – The Fire Dog – Essence of the day is Earth

If you have recently suffered the break-up of a relationship and you are not yet ready to move on, perhaps you should try to avoid being on your own this evening because the Constellation representing the poor Ox Boy makes another appearance. This may well encourage depression, but the best remedy for this is distraction, and the company of friends, family and loved ones can often play a crucial role, especially when we are feeling emotionally fragile. We all feel like this from time to time, for one reason or another, but if this applies to your present situation, don't sit around on your own tonight, get your address book out, get on the telephone and visit a friend.

Saturday November 25 – The Fire Pig – Essence of the day is Earth

The daily influences don't really agree with each other today, but that is not surprising because this is the last day of this lunar month and as a result, a time of no Moon. This often denotes secret, underhand dealings and it is difficult to see what can be achieved at times like this, apart from avoiding any unnecessary trouble. The best thing to do is to look on the bright side. The New Moon arrives tomorrow and with that, a fresh burst of rejuvenating energy, so the appropriate thing to do would be to spend a little time in preparation. It would be a good idea to clean and refresh any crystals you have in the home, and to have a good clean-out of the mind, body and spirit in order to be ready to absorb as much of the favourable energy as possible when the the New Moon arrives tomorrow.

Month 11

Sunday November 26 – The Earth Rat – Essence of the day is Fire

The New Moon arrives today to mark the beginning of the eleventh lunar month according to the Chinese calendar. The Almanac informs us that today is the day of cleansing and for sweeping away negative influences, so feng shui remedies are considered to be very effective today, although these should be confined to inside the home or business, because outside activities are not regarded as favourable. A perfect opportunity to spend some time recuperating, which could involve a bit of pleasant self-indulgence in the form of a massage or a visit to a leisure centre. Remember, we are in the Winter period now and this is the only opportunity that we have to replenish ourselves during the annual cycle and, arguably, the period when we should spoil ourselves the most.

Monday November 27 – The Earth Ox – Essence of the day is Fire

Today represents an opportunity for everyone to make a good start for the coming week, because all the signs point to success for those engaged in matters of importance. Keep this in mind as you look out of the bedroom window. The weather might not be very appealing but, with a nourishing breakfast inside you and a sparkle in your eyes, you can change your whole outlook on the day. Respected Master T'ung reminds us that the Emperor of Heaven is there to put money in everyone's pocket today and although, naturally, we are all expected to work for it, look on the bright side – at least we know that we will be paid today.

Tuesday November 28 – The Metal Tiger – Essence of the day is Wood

If you are still in full flow from yesterday, there is every reason to suggest that you can continue today with confidence because the influences favour continuity. Respected Master T'ung reminds us that today is the day of balance, so if you find yourself at a loose end, it would be wise to keep his comments in mind. Meditation and contemplation are both very much in harmony and they can be a wonderful source of replenishing energy, enabling us to cope with the many demands that are placed upon us. We all need to take time out now and again but sometimes circumstances don't allow for it. Today should offer you time to rest mind and body, so make use of the opportunity:

  When the mind is enlarged, the body is at ease.

Wednesday November 29 – The Metal Rabbit – Essence of the day is Wood

Today is another opportunity to acknowledge the work of Confucius; it is his festival today, so it would be very good feng shui to light a candle in his honour. A very auspicious day, even if it does encourage frantic activity, so it is an excellent time to acquire a new home or business, and it would also be wise to move into it today. Weddings are very favourable because the Almanac informs us that children born of a marriage today will bring honour and recognition to their parents, so imagine how proud the grandparents will be! Outside activities are also very much in harmony and if the weather is favourable, perhaps it would be wise to carry out any outdoor work that needs doing, since this would seem to be the appropriate time. Travel is also considered to be favourable, so at least everyone should be able to get around without too many problems.

Thursday November 30 – The Water Dragon – Essence of the day is Water

A day of mixed blessings really, it certainly won't be as frantic as yesterday, so try not to rush around at lightning speed because it will only be wasted energy, something that none of us can afford at this time of year. Try to direct your attention to matters in hand, and if you are at work, this applies to the more mundane, routine tasks that we need to attend to but often neglect. If you are at home, then you can utilise the favourable aspects by being productive and attending to any essential tasks around the home.

Friday December 1 – The Water Snake – Essence of the day is Water

The influences are very much in conflict today, because although Respected Master T'ung reminds us that this is the day of P'o, which translates as 'ruin' or 'defeat', the Constellation of the day is represented by Lou, which favours harmony and gatherings of all kinds. This may be due to the fact that it is also a day of celebration to the Jade Emperor himself and as a result, negative forces are in combat with the forces of good. However, if we all play our part, we should be able to tip the balance in favour of the good, and that way everyone can benefit. It is important to remember this today, because if you take a balanced view and see both sides of the equation, you are much more likely to make positive decisions. After all as the Chinese proverb reminds us:

 A fish on the wall has only one eye.

Saturday December 2 – The Wood Horse – Essence of the day is Metal

The best approach today is a light-hearted one because, although it is a fairly auspicious day, it has more connotations with leisure and pleasure than with academic or commercial success. An excellent night for a party, and if this happens to be a wedding reception, all the better, because not only will the bride and groom benefit from the proceedings, but the guests will as well. You don't need an excuse to party tonight – you will be going with the flow – and if it has been a while since you have tripped the light fantastic, then all the more reason to consider it tonight. So grab your partner or if they are not available, reach for the telephone and find out what everyone else is up to, because you may find out that you are not the only one who is thinking along these lines.

Sunday December 3 – The Wood Sheep – Essence of the day is Metal

It is not often that we have favourable aspects for travel on a Sunday, when many people are not working, and perhaps it would be smart to make use of this and treat the family to a day out. The influences are far too favourable to waste just lounging around the house, so it would be sensible to use the energy to exploit some of the many excellent leisure facilities that have become part of everyday life, but which few use to their full potential. You don't have to take the car, because at times like these other public forms of transport often work surprisingly well. The choice is yours; the main thing is to get out and enjoy yourself.

Monday December 4 – The Fire Monkey – Essence of the day is Fire

For those in business there is every reason to celebrate today, provided you are willing to play your part. An auspicious start to the week that encourages trading of all kinds, so whether you are buying or selling, you can really go with the flow today. For those wanting to get into business, perhaps looking for a suitable partner or seeking employment, there is equal cause for celebration, so not a time to be disillusioned. Think positive, act positive and look positive. Believe it or not, this is a day when you can succeed even against the odds. Appearance is important, so keep in mind the Chinese proverb:

A man is estimated by his clothes, a horse by his saddle.

Tuesday December 5 – The Fire Rooster – Essence of the day is Fire

If you have been suffering with a Winter cold or flu, then take heart, because today we are informed that the Heavenly Doctor is on duty, attending to the Emperor's messenger. As usual, he pays everyone a visit – we are all covered by Heaven's insurance policy, whether we like it or not. Respected Master T'ung advises us to catch up with any correspondence that we may have put to one side or forgotten about. It is always important to keep in touch with friends and family, irrespective of how far away they may live, so try to make full use of the technology available to contact somebody close to you. Family and friends are very important and can be a wonderful tonic as the following poem says:

> When sisters-in-law are joined in heart
> no family comes to ill.
> When sons all act a filial part
> it works like a harmony pill.

Wednesday December 6 – The Earth Dog – Essence of the day is Wood

Unfortunately there does not appear to be very much on offer today because once again we are informed that, to all intents and purposes, nature is closed for business. Taking into account that we are in the Winter period, this is more than a hint that you should not expect anything much from today and would be better off not pursuing rainbows. Take it easy, even if you are at work. Not even a top athlete can perform perfectly every day, and even if your boss expects a constantly high performance rate, he knows that in reality this is an impossible demand, so don't panic.

Thursday December 7 – The Earth Pig – Essence of the day is Wood

Today is the solar chi festival of Ta Hsueh, which translates as 'great snow', a natural progression from 'little snow', the previous festival, and this marks the first day of the second month of Winter. As the name suggests, this is a time when Winter really begins to take control and it is during this month that we experience the Winter solstice, the point at which the yin energy reaches its peak. After that, the seed of yang begins to grow, a comforting thought at this time of year when the weather and the Winter chi are both making their mark. So look on the bright side: Spring is not that far away even if the weather resembles conditions at the North Pole. Remember, hot food and rest work miracles at this time of year.

Friday December 8 – The Metal Rat – Essence of the day is Earth

We are reminded today to pay attention to our finances, pay our bills and chase up money that is owed to us, and this would be an excellent way to end the week. Although travel is fairly favourable, outside activities are not considered to be very auspicious, so if you are staying at home, try to stay inside and keep warm. Shopping is not considered to be very wise, because the temptation will be there to spend more than you can afford, so the smart thing to do would be to avoid the temptation and postpone that activity until you feel you are on a firmer foundation.

*Do not lean against a fence of bamboo sticks;
it is wiser to lean against a wall.*

Saturday December 9 – The Metal Ox – Essence of the day is Earth

It's a great day for sporting activities and even if you are not participating you can still go with the flow by making a contribution as a spectator. If the weather is favourable, an outside activity would be perfect as it will enable everyone to get a good blast of fresh air. So if you don't feel like jogging in the park, perhaps consider going to watch a game of football or visiting the race track – just the thing to blow the cobwebs away. Blast away the Winter blues by getting the adrenalin pumping and there is no better way than jumping up and down, cheering your head off!

Sunday December 10 – The Water Tiger – Essence of the day is Metal

Today is the day of the Full Moon, so emotions may be running a little higher than usual. Keep this in mind and make allowances accordingly. We all have moments when we are irrational and agitated and we should allow others the space to make the same mistakes, so please, have a little empathy. It is a good day for important meetings, functions and social events, so everyone should try to tap into these favourable influences and enjoy themselves as much as possible. The best way to do that is to encourage others to follow suit so that everyone can make contributions that will help to produce a real party atmosphere.

147

Monday December 11 – The Water Rabbit – Essence of the day is Metal

It would not be wise to attempt to rush into work and proceed full steam ahead today because the influences recommend a slow, deliberate and composed approach to the beginning of this week. Balance and harmony are the key words and we would all be wise to follow this advice given by Respected Master T'ung for our benefit. Going with the flow is the name of the game, and although Bob Dylan reminded us all that we don't need a weather man to know which way the wind is blowing, there are other influences, often much more subtle and as a result more difficult to detect, which can have an even more profound effect on our lives. It is these subtle energies that the Almanac was designed to tune us into, reminding us that they work in tandem with nature's natural energy cycles.

 The acts of high Heaven have neither sound nor smell.

Tuesday December 12 – The Wood Dragon – Essence of the day is Fire

Today is the birthday of O-me-t'o-fo, who is more commonly referred to as the Amitabha Buddha, a very important figure whose name means 'boundless light'. He is regarded in these terms because his teachings promoted the concept that nirvana could also be attained through faith – unlike the ideas of Sakyamuni, who felt that it could only be reached through the use of meditation. It would be very good feng shui to light a candle in his honour today as a mark of respect and as an acknowledgement of the light that he brought into this world, helping many to reach a greater understanding of their own faith.

Wednesday December 13 – The Wood Snake – Essence of the day is Fire

A fairly auspicious day, but not one that favours dashing around because travel is regarded as something to be avoided if possible. However, don't be fooled into thinking that we have all been given the day off, because this is not the case; in fact, we are reminded not only to work even harder than usual but also to direct our efforts closer to home. Domestic matters, not surprisingly, are considered to be very much in vogue today, so if you are stuck at home, try to play your part and use your time productively, because you won't always have such favourable conditions.

Thursday December 14 – The Fire Horse – Essence of the day is Water

Today is the Festival of the Nine Lotus Leaves, representing the nine realms of Buddhist philosophy, over which Kuan Yin, the goddess of mercy, is said to have control. If you make this the focus of your attention today, you will be much better equipped to deal with the negative influences that dominate the day. Respected Master T'ung advises us to avoid conflict and confrontation of any kind, and if you come across a situation where others express very different views from you, don't react in a negative or aggressive way. It would be much better if you keep in mind the example set by Kuan Yin and allow others the choice to be different.

Every sect has its doctrine and every doctrine has its sect.

Friday December 15 – The Fire Sheep – Essence of the day is Water

Although today represents a vast improvement on yesterday, it would be wise not to take any chances, because things just don't turn around that quickly. The best advice would be to try to focus on the small things, the routine tasks that don't require concentration and precision, because the chances are events won't necessarily go according to plan. If you plan for this and adjust your expectations accordingly, there should be no cause for disappointment and as a result, you should be insulated against any shocks. There is another week coming up, so there is no need to panic. The best course of action is to take things in your stride, because whatever needs doing it can always wait a little longer.

Saturday December 16 – The Earth Monkey – Essence of the day is Earth

A day of mixed fortunes but one that encourages activity, so the best advice is to keep busy, irrespective of whether you are at home or at work and even if you are out playing, so this is clearly a day to take seriously. Travel is considered to be fairly favourable, especially for those undertaking long journeys, although the Almanac advises against travelling by boat today because the omens indicate the possibility of shipwrecks. Outdoor activities are also considered to be favourable, so if the weather allows it, try to get some fresh air in order to take advantage of the positive energies.

FENG SHUI ALMANAC 2000

Sunday December 17 – The Earth Rooster – Essence of the day is Earth

If you are unhappy at the prospect of having to work today, then think again, because the portents are much more in harmony with those working than with those who are not. Look on the bright side, because although you may be forced to work, at least today you can prosper, which seems a fair exchange even if there are other things you would prefer to be doing. Travel is not considered to be particularly sensible and, as usual, if this cannot be avoided, it would be wise to take precautions, so if you are using public transport allow plenty of time and if you are driving, exercise additional caution.

Monday December 18 – The Metal Dog – Essence of the day is Metal

Today is considered to be the birthday of another one of the Eight Immortals, known as Chang Kuo, who is also considered to be the 'giver of sons'. His image is often seen on the beds of newly-weds to encourage male descendants. It is customary in China for couples to light candles in his honour today, especially if they are hoping to increase the family membership. On the family theme, Respected Master T'ung reminds us that it is time to catch up on any correspondence that may have been put to one side, especially any that involves friends, family or loved ones. It is important to remember birthdays, especially those of our parents, and this is emphasised by the words of Confucius:

> One should always remember the birthdays of one's parents because on one hand, their longevity is a cause of celebration but on the other hand, their old age is cause for concern.

Tuesday December 19 – The Metal Pig – Essence of the day is Metal

A day of mixed fortunes really, because although the Constellation of the day indicates the finding of hidden treasure, Respected Master T'ung reminds us that everything is closed for business today. With so much confusion, it would not be good to bank on anything, so go with the flow and wait and see what the day brings. If you are thinking of beginning a new diet, giving up smoking or starting some other new health regime, then the influences today will help to strengthen your resolve, so there is no need to wait until New Year's Eve – start today and by the time the New Year arrives, you will already be more than halfway there.

Wednesday December 20 – The Water Rat – Essence of the day is Wood

Try to be enthusiastic today because everything indicates that this is a very auspicious opportunity to begin to kick away the Winter blues. Tomorrow is the Winter solstice, the longest night of the year, but after that, the nights begin to get shorter and the days longer. Today encourages everyone to put the past behind them and to think about new ventures and opportunities that may present themselves over the coming year. With this in mind, everyone can be forgiven for spending at least part of the day contemplating future plans, hopes and dreams. Everything begins with a thought, and at this part of the year, when the yin energy is at its strongest, positive yang thoughts help to balance our attitudes.

Thursday December 21 – The Water Ox – Essence of the day is Wood

Today is the solar chi festival of Tung Chih, the Winter solstice, and this is a major festival for traditional Chinese families. At one time, tonight was considered to be New Year's Eve and even though this custom has changed, it is still a major event when all the family gather together in celebration. It has been described as a cross between Christmas Day and Thanksgiving, and certainly the emphasis is on the family as a unit. In ancient times this festival served as a focal point for the end of the year and a time when everyone would get together, often travelling huge distances in the process. It is worth remembering that in terms of nature's annual energy cycle, today marks a major turning point because from tomorrow the seed of yang begins to grow. It seems appropriate to end today with a Chinese poem, believed to have been written in the Tang Dynasty, around AD 800:

On our studies in the Springtime, it is hard to fix our minds,
while in incandescent Summer days, to sleep we feel inclined,
then the Autumn soon reminds us that the solstice must be near,
when we pack our bags and scramble home to welcome in the year.

Friday December 22 – The Wood Tiger – Essence of the day is Water

The influences today favour important events of all kinds, especially departing on holiday, which is considered to be very much in harmony with the day. Many people choose this time of year to have a holiday and in many ways it is very sensible, especially if you live in a place that has a severe Winter climate. There is no better way to replenish and rejuvenate ourselves than a holiday in the sun, especially during the Winter when the yin energy is at its peak. Even if you are not fortunate enough to be going on holiday today, try to retain that positive, enthusiastic approach, because opportunities will still come your way.

Saturday December 23 – The Wood Rabbit – Essence of the day is Water

A day of mixed fortunes, although if you are in full flow then you don't really have anything to worry about. Only those with itchy feet need to proceed with caution. Respected Master T'ung reminds us that it is a day of equal gathering and dividing, which denotes that it is a good opportunity to reflect on our actions. Balance is the key to harmony and it would be very appropriate to contemplate the coming year and to look at ways to improve not only our lives, but also the lives of others as well. One way in which we can all participate is to encourage others by sharing our knowledge and experience.

Sunday December 24 – The Fire Dragon – Essence of the day is Earth

It is Christmas Eve and if you find yourself rushing around doing last-minute shopping, at least you have the benefit of the influences supporting you. Alternatively, you may well be at home, making all the necessary preparations for the coming celebrations, in which case you are every bit as busy and therefore still going with the flow. Activity is the key word today and it would be foolish to waste this opportunity, especially on Christmas Eve when there is always so much still to be done, even with the best preparation in the world. As always, balance is the key and if we are fortunate enough to have the resources to spoil our friends, family and loved ones, it would be very good feng shui to consider those less fortunate than ourselves. Christmas should be about the joy of giving and not tainted by commercialism.

Monday December 25 – The Fire Snake – Essence of the day is Earth

It's Christmas Day and I would like to wish everyone a very merry Christmas! I hope that today brings happiness and peace to everyone. It is appropriate that the portents indicate that the emphasis is on the home today, a place where many people will be spending their time in the company of friends and family. A day that favours the very young, who relish the thought of opening their presents and who are often so excited they have difficulty in containing themselves. Don't worry if they are too busy to show their appreciation. It's not that they don't care, it's just that they are too involved with all the excitement, so keep in mind the humorous view of the Chinese, expressed in the following proverb:

 There are only affectionate fathers and mothers, there are no affectionate children.

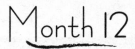

Month 12

Tuesday December 26 – The Earth Horse – Essence of the day is Fire

As always with a new lunar month, it begins with the New Moon and with it a fresh burst of rejuvenating energy. This should add an additional boost of optimism, promoting an even greater sense of goodwill to all – appropriate sentiments at all times but even more so during the Christmas period. This approach will pay dividends today, because, unfortunately, not all the portents are auspicious, so go with the flow and enjoy the Christmas festivities. Family, friends and loved ones are all highlighted by the Almanac today and the only word of caution concerns alcohol intake – take it easy, because any abuse will only result in the negative aspects of conflict and confrontation presenting themselves in one way or another.

Wednesday December 27 – The Earth Sheep – Essence of the day is Fire

The worst of the negative aspects have now passed and everyone can look forward to a more prosperous, happy period, so be enthusiastic and positive and go with the flow. Respected Master T'ung urges us all to be in a joyous mood, so don't invite trouble by tackling anything awkward or difficult – enjoy yourself! If that involves putting your feet up and resting in between bouts of eating and drinking, so be it. Not only is it Winter, a time when we should eat and sleep more, it is also Christmas, so relax and indulge yourself; there could not be a more appropriate time to 'go the whole hog' or as the Chinese sometimes prefer to say:

 Cook a Dragon and kill a Phoenix.

Thursday December 28 – The Metal Monkey – Essence of the day is Wood

An auspicious day in many respects and one that encourages us to visit friends and family because everything points to hassle-free travel today, so it would seem sensible to make use of these beneficial influences. Outside activities are also very favourable, so if you need fresh air after the recent celebrations, today provides a good opportunity to go for a walk, potter around the garden or enjoy any other outdoor activity. It would be wise to keep active, because after putting our feet up for a while we need to get our circulation going again.

Friday December 29 – The Metal Rooster – Essence of the day is Wood

Another day that favours activity of all kinds, so if you are already back at work, try to get into the swing of things as quickly as possible since the chances are it's going to be a very hectic but prosperous day. Trading in general is considered to be very appropriate today, even in conjunction with the use of savings, so if you are attending any sales or auctions, keep your eyes open – there are sure to be some bargains available. Mind you, this should not be taken as a licence to spend, spend, spend; just think of it as an assurance that if you do decide to make an investment today, at least you have selected the right time. All you need to do is to be in the right place, which may prove difficult, since travel is not considered to be very favourable, so a good tip would be to try to stay close to home.

Saturday December 30 – The Water Dog – Essence of the day is Water

Another very auspicious day that should encourage everyone to adopt an enthusiastic, positive approach. The Heavenly Doctor is on duty, so those recuperating should receive an additional boost today and everyone can achieve something by making an effort – even fun should be treated seriously today. Respected Master T'ung informs us that it would be very appropriate to contact friends, family and loved ones, so get your address book out and make use of the telephone. On days like today, there is no telling what opportunities may come your way and if you go with the flow and make an effort to contact others, you improve the chances of benefits coming your way.

Sunday December 31 – The Water Pig – Essence of the day is Water

Here in the Western world, today is New Year's Eve and a day when many people will be out celebrating, because this is arguably the biggest party night of the year. It may well feel a little tame after last year's millennium celebrations, but this does not mean that tonight will be any less enjoyable. In fact with less hype and less build-up, the chances of disappointment are much reduced. The portents are not particularly suited for large gatherings and this offers the opportunity for a more peaceful, family-oriented celebration. This may well suit many people, especially those who were not really happy with the activities of last year, but the best advice for everyone is to go with the flow and enjoy whatever you do.

Monday January 1 – The Wood Rat – Essence of the day is Metal

For many people today is a holiday but if for any reason you are at work, then don't worry – the influences of the day favour activity. Another aspect of the daily influences which is very appropriate is the fact that they encourage anyone who has made a New Year's resolution, irrespective of what that was, as long as it was designed to be of benefit. Travel is not particularly good today, so if this is unavoidable, take the usual precautions and be prepared for delays, congestion and all the other negative aspects of travel that often manifest themselves when it doesn't flow smoothly.

Tuesday January 2 – The Wood Ox – Essence of the day is Metal

Feng shui remedies are well favoured today: Respected Master T'ung reminds us that this is a day to sweep away negative influences and obstacles. Good advice at the best of times, but even more appropriate at this time of year when we are all looking for a fresh start. If you are at home today, have a look around and see how much clutter has been accumulated over the last few days and spend a little time getting rid of it to freshen up the home. Open the windows, clean the bathroom, vacuum the lounge – you know, all those boring, mundane tasks that have to be attended to from time to time – but today everybody in the house should be encouraged to join in. Even children and young people can play their part and if they are willing, as an additional incentive, the Almanac informs us that there will be bonus points available for those who really make an effort.

Wednesday January 3 – The Fire Tiger – Essence of the day is Fire

Today is the festival of Ju-Lai Buddha, which commemorates the time when Buddha Sakyamuni, or Gautama Buddha as he is known as outside China, achieved enlightenment. Today is therefore a very important festival for Buddhists. Anyone who has a statue of Buddha, in any shape or form, should light a candle in his honour today as a mark of respect. It may well be good feng shui to have statues of Buddha around the home, but that being the case, it cannot be good feng shui to forget occasions like today. The portents look very favourable, so there is no reason why everybody should not benefit and all we have to do is to make an effort and participate, which, on reflection, seems a very reasonable deal.

Thursday January 4 – The Fire Rabbit – Essence of the day is Fire

If you find yourself in the middle of things, whatever you do, don't stop, because the influences today favour those who complete their tasks. If you are at a loose end, then take some time out to reflect because Respected Master T'ung urges us all to spend a little time, at least, in quiet, meditative thought. Remember that it is the Winter and at this time of the year we should be trying to store our vitality so that we are ready to leap into action when Spring arrives. Preparation is very important and rest and recuperation are integral parts of that process, which involves storing vital resources to achieve an objective, whatever that may be.

 A job considered beforehand presents fewer obstacles.

Friday January 5 – The Earth Dragon – Essence of the day is Wood

Today is the solar chi festival of Hsiao Han, which can be interpreted as 'little cold', and this marks the beginning of the last month of Winter. As the name suggests, this is a time when the weather changes again, with the emphasis on the word 'cold' and it is nature's way of saying that it gets worse before it gets better. This is the last surge of the Winter chi before we can benefit from the new Spring energy, so it is not surprising that Winter ends with a flourish – such a powerful force is hardly going to go out with a whimper. Another good day to adjust ourselves and to nurture and conserve our vitality, so chill out and relax, because it will not pay to rush around too much today.

Saturday January 6 – The Earth Snake – Essence of the day is Wood

A day of mixed fortunes that will favour those who try to focus on their own affairs and stay out of other people's business. There is an indication of sadness and as a result it would not be wise to expect too much today, especially in matters of importance, but that should not be used as an excuse not to make an effort, because once again the emphasis is on activity. We are reminded by Respected Master T'ung to avoid making accusations; something which we should try to avoid at all times, but even more so when the Almanac warns against it. So go about your business with a happy, enthusiastic approach and encourage others to adopt the same attitude.

Sunday January 7 – The Metal Horse – Essence of the day is Earth

It would not be wise to dash around too much today – for one thing, the influences do not favour travel. Sunday is traditionally a day of rest and if this appeals to you, then you should take advantage of the opportunity. If others around you are busy, don't let them make you feel guilty if you want to relax; and if you are feeling active, don't expect others to be as well. Everyone has the right to get into their own rhythm, especially at this time of the year when the object of the exercise is to store and nurture our vitality, not to achieve maximum productivity. Domestic matters are considered to be very favourable today and if you are feeling active, look around the home for something to do, but don't use this an excuse to make demands on others. Go with the flow and leave others the opportunity to do the same.

Monday January 8 – The Metal Sheep – Essence of the day is Earth

A variable start to the week, which encourages a gentle approach, so it would be sensible to ease yourself gently into your routine and not take the swashbuckling approach, so leave the Errol Flynn suit at home today. Diplomacy is the name of the game, especially if faced with any kind of confrontation, because otherwise things may well escalate out of control. Empathy and understanding are very powerful tools against negative, aggressive energy and sometimes it only takes a few kind words to diffuse a potentially explosive situation – although often in the heat of the moment it is the last thing we think of. We all put on our protective clothing now and again, and there is nothing wrong in that, but we should not forget that it is only a disguise. Keep in mind the Chinese proverb that says:

 With the body of a sheep clothed in a tiger's skin, merit can never be achieved.

Tuesday January 9 – The Water Monkey – Essence of the day is Metal

Today is the day of the Full Moon and it is also considered to be the birthday of Sage Wan, a famous general who was deified. It would be very good feng shui to light a candle in his honour today, because this is also considered to be a very appropriate time to celebrate the occupants of Heaven and to offer up prayers to the gods. A day to be happy and go with the flow, so don't make life difficult for yourself; there are plenty of other influences capable of doing that and your job today is to make life as easy as possible. If this involves treating yourself in some way or taking time out to be on your own, then so be it, because you have a choice, so exercise that right and enjoy it.

Wednesday January 10 – The Water Rooster – Essence of the day is Metal

An auspicious day in every respect and one which everyone should try to utilise to the best of their ability. Travel is considered to be very favourable, so there is an opportunity to make use of the transport system to maximum effect. If you have places to go and people to see, today provides the ideal opportunity. Weddings are considered to be very auspicious today – the Almanac informs us that they will produce talented children who will bring joy and honour to their parents. Although marriage these days appears to be a risky affair, especially in the West where divorce is all too common, things can change only if we make an effort. The best thing we can do is to encourage optimism and hope and to make an effort to try to reverse the trend. If you are getting married today, sweep away all negative thoughts because you can make it work.

Thursday January 11 – The Wood Dog – Essence of the day is Fire

Another day that favours activity of all kinds, so however bad the weather, don't let it get you down. Put your best foot forward and brave the day. A good breakfast under your belt should help to set you up for the day and if you combine this with an enthusiastic and positive approach, you can be sure that you have at least half a chance of success. Outside activities are also considered to be favourable so it doesn't really matter if you are at home or at work, inside or outside, there should be something to suit everyone. The only word of caution relates to travel. Try to avoid it if you can, or at the very least, make allowances, because any journey undertaken today may well take a lot longer than expected.

Friday January 12 – The Wood Pig – Essence of the day is Fire

The daily influences indicate a natural conclusion to the week and if you are at work or in business, then you should bear this in mind and try to tie up as many loose ends as possible. If you are at home, try to use this opportunity to have a good clear-out, because this will enable you to make a fresh start next week. Respected Master T'ung suggests that it would be appropriate to attend to any correspondence that has been put to one side, especially if it is connected with friends or family. Music and the arts are also very well favoured today and no doubt there will be some extremely good performances this evening. Anyone who makes the effort to attend a performance will certainly not regret it, because it is not only the performers who benefit today, but everyone involved.

Saturday January 13 – The Fire Rat – Essence of the day is Water

Not the most auspicious of days but a time when we have to make the best of it and remember that there is always something good to be recycled from any situation, however negative it may seem. The best course of action is to make life easy for yourself and avoid competing with anyone or anything. Not only is it a waste of energy, it is also futile, because at the end of the day we only really compete with ourselves and at this time of the year the object is to store vital resources, not spend them. The first rule in learning to go with the flow is to be in harmony with the seasons, and this means adjusting your cycles of rest and activity to be in harmony with nature's natural energy cycles. Failure to do this results in a situation that the Chinese proverb describes as:

Like the man who goes hawking with an owl,
the man and the bird are well matched.

Sunday January 14 – The Fire Ox – Essence of the day is Water

Today is considered by many to be another festival to commemorate the imperial carpenter Luo Pan and it would be very good feng shui to light a candle in honour of the home. This applies particularly to those involved in the construction industry because he is also considered to be the Chinese equivalent of the patron saint of builders. The portents are very favourable today, encouraging not only harmony and happiness in the home but also success and prosperity in business by stimulating new ideas and ventures. The Winter Earth season will soon be here and this reminds us that Spring is on its way, so there is every reason to feel optimistic about the future. Enjoy the day and encourage others to do the same.

Monday January 15 – The Earth Tiger – Essence of the day is Earth

Unfortunately, if you had planned to get your week off to a flying start, then you must think again, because the influences do not favour this approach. Respected Master T'ung reminds us that this is another one of those days when we should all clear away negative influences from our lives, whether they are emotional, physical or spiritual, because on the path to the future there is no room for these obstacles. Health is one of the most important aspects at this time of the year, when really we should devote as much time and energy as possible to overhauling ourselves and our environment in readiness for the activity to come. So blow away those Winter blues, get rid of those negative thoughts and start planning your future.

Tuesday January 16 – The Earth Rabbit – Essence of the day is Earth

An auspicious day today that will enable everything to flow much more smoothly. If you spent yesterday preparing the ground, you should now be in a position to go forward, full steam ahead. Important events of all kinds are favoured today, so whether you are applying for a job or getting married, the influences are supporting you. This is a day to be confident and to look beyond boring, routine tasks that we all have to deal with and focus on more important issues. We all have the power to change our lives for the better, but in order to do this, it is necessary to make that leap into the next cycle. On days like today, these leaps can be made, but only by making an effort and seizing opportunities when they present themselves, so reach for the stars because anything less just will not do.

Wednesday January 17 – The Metal Dragon – Essence of the day is Metal

Today is the beginning of the Winter Earth season, a period which nature provides for us to adjust and realign ourselves to ensure that we stay on track. It is a balancing period which we should all try to utilise to prepare ourselves for the coming Spring and the activity that brings. Hibernation should now be coming to an end and over the next few weeks, the objective is to prepare the ground for the coming year. In traditional Chinese homes, candles are lit and incense is burnt as an offering to the kitchen god, because at midnight he leaves to make his report to the Jade Emperor. Today provides us with an opportunity to give him messages in the hope that he will pass them on to Heaven, enabling all our hopes, dreams and aspirations to come to fruition, so light candles and give thanks for our home, our friends and our loved ones. There is a lovely poem concerning the kitchen god, which is very appropriate at this time of year.

Come god of the kitchen whose surname is Chang,
now here is your pudding and here is your T'ang.
When you arrive in Heaven it will make us all glad,
if you tell what is good and omit what is bad.

Thursday January 18 – The Metal Snake – Essence of the day is Metal

Another day that favours all kinds of activity and if you are at home today, it would be wise to focus your efforts on the kitchen. The reason for this is that since the kitchen god makes his report to the Jade Emperor today, concerning the behaviour of the family over the past year, the Emperor may wish to look in and make a personal inspection. That being the case, it would be wise to make the best impression possible and there is no better way to do this than to have a clean, warm and inviting kitchen, which is the 'heart' of the home. The paper image of the kitchen god is often smeared with honey, some say to stick his lips together to prevent him from speaking, others to sweeten him up, encouraging a good report. The paper is then burnt, allowing it to ascend to Heaven, and at the Chinese New Year, a new image is put up to serve as a reminder that there is always someone watching over us.

Friday January 19 – The Water Horse – Essence of the day is Wood

The Ox Boy makes his last appearance for the year and if you have recently separated from your partner, then you may feel a little more fragile than usual. Try to put it behind you. Spring is on its way and with it the opportunity for new beginnings. The daily influences encourage work around the home, with the emphasis placed firmly on domestic duties, so anyone at home should take note and make sure they are taking their share of the responsibility. Travel is not viewed well today, so try to find things to do nearer to home if possible. Long journeys are likely to be fraught with difficultes.

Saturday January 20 – The Water Sheep – Essence of the day is Wood

Today is the solar chi festival of Ta Han, which translates as meaning 'great cold', marking the last solar fortnight of Winter, and, as the name suggests, mother nature has saved the coldest weather until last. The good news, of course, is that Spring is just around the corner, but in the meantime it is important to stay warm, eat well and get plenty of rest, because although there is work to do, the real business of the year hasn't yet started. Conserve your energy as much as possible and start gradually to prepare the ground so that the seeds of Spring have a better environment in which to flourish.

Sunday January 21 – The Wood Monkey – Essence of the day is Water

Another day to go with the flow and it is appropriate that today is Sunday, when many people get a break from work, because the day favours those who do what pleases them. There is no point in trying to get others to fit in with your plans, so the smart thing to do is to consider yourself and do what you want to do. Of course, this also includes allowing others the same freedom and so even if you don't want to exercise your right to choose, you should not prevent others from doing so. Give everyone a little rope to express themselves in their own way, especially family and friends.

 The tiger, though fierce, does not devour its cubs.

FENG SHUI ALMANAC 2000

Monday January 22 – The Wood Rooster – Essence of the day is Water

An auspicious day in many respects and one that many traditional Chinese families use to get together to forgive and forget the differences of the last year. This is in preparation for the Chinese New Year and it is believed that on this day the North Star descends to Earth to judge the actions of everyone here. The Chinese believe that it is not harmonious to begin a New Year with grudges and resentment, and it is in the interests of everyone to forgive each other and start again with a clean slate. We all make mistakes, but if we cannot forgive others, we cannot expect anyone to forgive us. There are those who believe in 'an eye for an eye', but I favour another approach, which I first came across many years ago in the form of a piece of graffiti, which I shall always remember:

 An eye for an eye and in the end the world goes blind.

Tuesday January 23 – The Fire Dog – Essence of the day is Earth

Today is Chinese New Year's Eve and for many this is a day of preparation in readiness for the coming celebrations. Tomorrow represents another opportunity to push your life forward in a positive direction and to put the past behind you. It may well be that the coming year will bring you happiness and prosperity, especially if things have not been going well in recent years, because eventually things change for the better. This is a time to be optimistic about the future and to consider what you want out of life: we all have the ability to change it, however desperate our situation appears to be. It only takes one twist of fate to make that leap into a more positive, happy and harmonious cycle, but the difficult thing is to be able to recognise it when it appears. Remain positive and keep your 'radar' on at all times, because you never quite know when it will happen.

Introducing the Portents

Over the last three years, feng shui has become very popular and a large number of books have been published to help readers to practise feng shui for themselves. The concept of favourable directions and areas within the home is very ancient and in the *Li Chi,* or *Book of Rites and Ceremony,* there is information relating to the Emperor and his palace, which forms the basis of many styles of feng shui.

These 'palaces' or 'portents' are used in a variety of ways, depending on the style of feng shui adopted, but many people will be aware of the names of these influences because they are often used to describe favourable and unfavourable directions. In the *Li Chi,* they are referred to as 'areas' within the Emperor's palace, which is divided into nine equal squares and arranged in the same way as the Lo Shu.

Although there are nine squares, the central square and the square that contains the main door are considered to be neutral. As a result, both these areas are thought to be reasonably favourable.

The names of the seven major portents and their meanings are:

- Nien Yen: long life
- Sheng Chi: the source of chi
- T'ien I: celestial monad, or heavenly doctor
- Hai Huo: accidents and mishaps
- Chueh Ming: broken fate
- Wu Kuei: five ghosts
- Liu Sha: six imps or six curses.

Like the flying stars, these portents are also said to fly around different areas according to the direction in which the main door of the house faces, and they offer a good starting point to seeing how feng shui can affect your home. By looking at the chart that represents the direction your front door faces, you can see what areas of your home are influenced by which portents.

Nien Yen – Long Life

This is the perfect area for the main bedroom but it is also suitable for the living room, a work room or another bedroom. This space should be used as much as possible since it is a very favourable influence.

Sheng Chi – Source of Chi

Since this area is full of energy, this is another place which should be utilised to the full, and this makes it an ideal location for an office or work room for someone who works from home. Artists, painters, musicians and writers would all benefit from working in this area.

T'ien I – Heavenly Doctor

This area represents the ideal location for rest and recuperation, so whether you have suffered emotionally, physically, spiritually or financially, this is the area to spend as much time in as possible in order to repair, rejuvenate and refresh yourself.

Hai Huo – Accidents and Mishaps

As the name suggests, this area is associated with accidents, and if possible this location should not be used for anything which may be affected by this. Not the ideal place for a small child's bedroom, the kitchen or a work room, for example, because clearly these are all prone to accidents anyway.

Chueh Ming – Broken Fate

This is considered to be by far the worst of the portents and one that should be avoided as a bedroom, especially if the person sleeping there is suffering from an illness. In an ideal world, this area would be used only for storage. Of course, we don't all live in an ideal world, so if you do find that you have no choice but to position important rooms in this area, you can minimise the negative effects. Firstly, if the area comes under a favourable flying star, and this is very likely to be the case, this will already be diminishing the negative aspects. However, you can also identify which element is associated with that area and introduce more of the supporting element, according to the cycle of generation (see page 167).

Wu Kuei – Five Ghosts

This area is often used for the family shrine because, as the name suggests, it is associated with ghosts and spirits. An ideal location for a medium or clairvoyant to utilise for providing home readings for clients.

Liu Sha – Six Imps or Six Curses

This is not as bad as it sounds because it is only really associated with minor setbacks that keep recurring. There is not a lot that can be done, apart from being aware of this so that you can try to avoid repeated mistakes. If you do find yourself quarrelling here, however, avoid this area of the home if there is potential for conflict.

Introducing the Flying Stars

These are another tool that many feng shui masters use to incorporate the time element into their calculations, and since feng shui is said to fluctuate in natural rhythms, where nothing can stay perfect all the time, feng shui is very much concerned with both time and space.

The Emperor was said to move around his palace during the course of the year in order to tap into the influences that he most needed at any particular time, as well as to avoid negative energy. Although most of us don't have that luxury, we can still make use of the temporal aspect of the feng shui calculations.

There are Nine Stars, which are associated with the nine stars of the Great Bear, or the Plough as we often call it, including the Pole Star or North Star, to which the Plough points. They also relate to the nine squares of the Lo Shu and for that reason they are often called by the number and colour associated with them. Like the portents, some are considered to be favourable and some not. There are many different styles of feng shui and each one uses different applications, but this book provides a sound, basic introduction to the most common concepts. Becoming a feng shui master takes many years of dedication, study and experience.

The Stars			
1	White	Water	Lucky
2	Black	Earth	Unlucky
3	Jade	Wood	Can be lucky or unlucky
4	Green	Wood	Lucky
5	Yellow	Earth	Unlucky
6	White	Metal	Lucky
7	Red	Metal	Can be lucky or unlucky
8	White	Earth	Lucky
9	Purple	Fire	Can be lucky or unlucky

Using the Flying Star Charts

The following pages contain eight sets of charts that relate to the eight directions in which the front door of the house may face. It is not by any means a definitive approach to feng shui, but if you are a beginner, this is a great place to start: not only is it fairly easy to grasp, but it is also based on very sound principles, as laid out in the Chinese classics.

Many systems of feng shui use methods to provide a birth chart for the house based on the Ruling Star for the period when the house was built. Other systems use combinations of stars for the back door as well as the front, and there are yet more systems that use a combination of these and other factors as well. I therefore stress that this assessment is merely a starting point for the beginner, although a very good and useful one which hopefully will inspire you to experiment at home and make you want to find out more about this fascinating subject. For those interested in studying this further I would recommend reading *The Feng Shui Handbook* by Derek Walters (Thorsons), *Feng Shui* by Raymond Lo (Times Publishing) and *Feng Shui, the Ancient Wisdom of Harmonious Living for Modern Times* by Eva Wong (Shambala).

How to Use the Charts

Turn to the pages relating to the direction in which the main door of your house faces. All the individual charts are aligned with the correct compass direction in relation to the position of the front door on the charts, so that on the charts for the house facing north, the position where the door is marked is north. On the following charts for the house facing north-east, the position where the door is marked is north-east, and so on.

The first chart gives you an indication of the general portents associated with that particular house. In more detailed studies, these portents can also be said to move around the house.

The second and third charts show the Ruling Star for the year, with the other nine stars arranged according to their appropriate directions. This represents the general picture of your home for the year. From these charts, you will be able to see which areas of the home are occupied by which star, and this will denote whether an area is favourable or not over the coming year.

The remaining charts show how the stars also fly around on a monthly basis, so in each case, the main number in each square is the star associated with that area of the house for that lunar month. The number in the centre square is the Ruling Star for that month, and these remain the same whatever direction your house is facing. The Ruling Star for the month is therefore fixed, and the other stars fly round it according to the direction of the front door.

The monthly movement of the stars combine with the annual arrangement of the stars to form combinations, and the smaller numbers in each square are the relevant stars for that area for the whole year. The main number and the smaller number in each square therefore show you the combination for the month. Naturally, certain combinations are said to be more favourable than others and you can use this to your benefit (see page 168).

Feng Shui Remedies

You can use feng shui remedies to stimulate the positive energies in your home, and there are recommendations in the diary pages for days that are particularly favourable for this kind of activity.

The golden rule for remedies generally is to remember the two governing cycles of the five elements and the fact that, as usual, balance is the key.

The elements are linked in a positive combination of energies, moving through a repeating cycle. Wood generates fire, which in turn generates Earth, which generates Metal, which generates Water, which then generates Wood, and so on. This is the cycle of generation, sometimes known as the compatibility or positive cycle.

In balance with this is the cycle of destruction or incompatibility cycle. Fire controls Metal, which controls Wood, which controls Earth, which controls Water, which controls Fire. If Fire represents a problem, therefore, the best treatment is to introduce actual or symbolic Water features, since Water is said to control Fire.

Using these basic principles and identifying the element associated with the flying star (see page 165) will show you which element supports and which element controls the prevailing star in each case. If you want to diminish the power of an unfavourable star, all you need to do is to introduce something that is associated with the element that controls the star.

There are other remedies that have become very popular. If you want to try to experiment with wind chimes, then use the areas that are under the influence of favourable combinations in order to activate that highly auspicious energy. Of course, you should remember to take them down at the appropriate time before the influence changes, otherwise you may well activate something that would be best left undisturbed.

Lucky money frogs are becoming very popular and these can be used to activate wealth luck when good combinations occur. If you have a wealth and money combination by your front door in any month, then placing the frog there, just for that month, would enhance its money-making attributes. Alternatively, if you have a frog in the house which happens to be in a position where the money luck is not good, you would be better to move it to another position where it can be of service.

Strings of lucky Chinese coins can be used in the same way, but they are at their most effective when luck is running with them.

The Combinations

Naturally, certain combinations are said to be more favourable than others. Look at the following section on remedies to see what action you can take in order to maximise the effects of the positive energies.

Education, Study and Learning – Combinations of Six and One
The combination of six and one is said to govern influences associated with learning, and when this combination appears in the north, it is particularly auspicious, although it is also favourable when it appears in the east or south-east. Both six and one are associated with Metal, so the introduction of the Earth element in the area will activate it further. However, when it appears in the south, it can denote that the head of the house will suffer in some way, so introduce Water to control southern Fire.

Financial Success – Combinations of Two and Seven
The combination of two and seven is said to govern finances and is at its most powerful when it appears in the south. Two and seven are associated with Earth and Metal and the introduction of the Fire element would boost this interaction, since Fire generates Earth, which generates Metal. The south-west and the north-east are also favourable for this combination but caution is needed when it appears in the west or north-west.

Status, Credibility and Advantage – Combinations of Three and Eight
The combination of three and eight is said to rule over these aspects and is at its most powerful when it appears in the east or the south-east. The south is also a favourable position for this combination but it should be treated with caution when it appears in the south-west.

Career and Business – Combinations of Four and Nine
The combination of four and nine is said to rule over the aspects of career and business in our lives and is most at home when it appears in the west or north-west. It is also comfortable in the north. Only when it appears in the east is there reason to be careful.

Fame – Combinations of Four and Six
The combination of four and six denotes fame, and you can introduce the Water element to help improve this Metal and Wood combination and really make it go with the flow.

Family Harmony and Celebration – Combinations of Eight and Nine
The combination of eight and nine denotes family harmony and celebration and this can be enhanced by the introduction of the Wood element.

Sickness – Combinations of Five and Two
The combination of five and two denotes sickness, but since both these numbers are associated with the Earth element, introducing the Wood element into this area would help to balance the negative effects.

Problems in Business – Combinations of Two and Nine
The combination of two and nine suggests problems in business, but this Fire and Earth combination can be balanced out by the introduction of Water.

FLYING STARS FOR 1999

9	5	7
8	1	3
4	6	2

FLYING STARS FOR 2000

8	4	6
7	9	2
3	5	1

PORTENTS

SHENG CHI SOURCE OF CHI	NIEN YEN LONG LIFE	CHUEH MING BROKEN FATE
T'IEN I HEAVENLY DOCTOR	DOOR FACES NORTH ↓	HAI HUO ACCIDENTS
WU KUEI FIVE GHOSTS		LIU SHA SIX IMPS

MONTH 10 1999
November 8–December 7

7 ⁹	3 ⁵	5 ⁷
6 ⁸	8 ¹	1 ³
2 ⁴	☆ 4 ⁶	9 ²

MONTH 11 1999
December 8–January 6

6 ⁹	✚ 2 ⁵	4 ⁷
5 ⁸	7 ¹	9 ³
1 ⁴	3 ⁶	8 ²

MONTH 12 1999
January 7–February 4

5 ⁹	1 ⁵	3 ⁷
4 ⁸	📖 6 ¹	🏵 8 ³
💰 9 ⁴	2 ⁶	💰 7 ²
		CAUTION

 Education, study and learning
 Financial success

 Status, credibility and advantage
 Career and business

MONTH 1 2000
February 5–March 5

4 [8] 🛍️	9 [4]	2 [6]
3 [7]	5 [9]	7 [2] 🪵 **CAUTION**
8 [3] 🏅	1 [5]	6 [1] 📖

MONTH 2 2000
March 6–April 4

3 [8] 🏅 **VERY GOOD**	8 [4]	1 [6] 📖
2 [7] 🪵	4 [9] 🛍️	6 [2]
7 [3]	9 [5]	5 [1]

MONTH 3 2000
April 5–May 3

2 [8]	7 [4]	9 [6]
1 [7]	3 [9]	5 [2] ✚
6 [3]	8 [5]	4 [1]

MONTH 4 2000
May 4–June 1

1 [8]	6 [4] 🌟	8 [6]
9 [7]	2 [9] 🏚️	4 [2]
5 [3]	7 [5]	3 [1]

MONTH 5 2000
June 2–July 1

9 [8] 🍾	5 [4]	7 [6]
8 [7]	1 [9]	3 [2]
4 [3]	6 [5]	2 [1]

MONTH 6 2000
July 2–July 30

8 [8]	4 [4]	6 [6]
7 [7]	9 [9]	2 [2]
3 [3]	5 [5]	1 [1]

🌟 Fame

🍾 Family harmony and celebration

170

✚ Sickness

🏚️ Problems in business

MONTH 7 2000
July 31–August 28

7 [8]	3 [4]	5 [6]
6 [7]	🥂 8 [9]	1 [2]
2 [3]	4 [5]	9 [1]

MONTH 8 2000
August 29–September 27

6 [8]	2 [4]	✴ 4 [6]
5 [7]	7 [9]	🎴 9 [2]
1 [3]	3 [5]	8 [1]

MONTH 9 2000
September 28–October 26

5 [8]	1 [4]	3 [6]
4 [7]	6 [9]	8 [2]
9 [3]	✚ 2 [5]	7 [1]

MONTH 10 2000
October 27–November 25

4 [8] 📁	9 [4]	2 [6]
3 [7]	5 [9]	🪙 7 [2] **CAUTION**
🏅 8 [3]	1 [5]	📖 6 [1]

MONTH 11 2000
November 26–December 25

🏅 3 [8] **VERY GOOD**	8 [4]	📖 1 [6]
🪙 2 [7]	📁 4 [9]	6 [2]
7 [3]	9 [5]	5 [1]

MONTH 12 2000
December 26–January 23

2 [8]	7 [4]	9 [6]
1 [7]	3 [9]	✚ 5 [2]
6 [3]	8 [5]	4 [1]

📖 Education, study and learning

🪙 Financial success

171

🏅 Status, credibility and advantage

📁 Career and business

FLYING STARS FOR 1999

5	7	3
9	1	2
8	4	6

FLYING STARS FOR 2000

4	6	2
8	9	1
7	3	5

PORTENTS

HAI HUO ACCIDENTS	**SHENG CHI** SOURCE OF CHI	**NIEN YEN** LONG LIFE
CHUEH MING BROKEN FATE	**DOOR FACES NORTH EAST** ↓	**T'IEN I** HEAVENLY DOCTOR
LIU SHA SIX IMPS		**WU KUEI** FIVE GHOSTS

MONTH 10 1999
November 8–December 7

3 ⁵	5 ⁷	1 ³
7 ⁹	8 ¹	🀫 9 ²
6 ⁸	2 ⁴	✨ 4 ⁶

MONTH 11 1999
December 8–January 6

➕ 2 ⁵	4 ⁷	9 ³
6 ⁹	7 ¹	8 ²
5 ⁸	1 ⁴	3 ⁶

MONTH 12 1999
January 7–February 4

1 ⁵	3 ⁷	🏵 8 ³
5 ⁹ 📖	6 ¹	🍵 7 ² **CAUTION**
4 ⁸ 🛍	9 ⁴	2 ⁶

✨ Fame

👯 Family harmony and celebration

➕ Sickness

🀫 Problems in business

MONTH 1 2000
February 5–March 5

9 ⁴	2 ⁶	7 ² CAUTION
4 ⁸	5 ⁹	6 ¹
3 ⁷	8 ³	1 ⁵

MONTH 2 2000
March 6–April 4

8 ⁴	1 ⁶	6 ²
3 ⁸ VERY GOOD	4 ⁹	5 ¹
2 ⁷	7 ³	9 ⁵

MONTH 3 2000
April 5–May 3

7 ⁴	9 ⁶	5 ²
2 ⁸	3 ⁹	4 ¹
1 ⁷	6 ³	8 ⁵

MONTH 4 2000
May 4–June 1

6 ⁴	8 ⁶	4 ²
1 ⁸	2 ⁹	3 ¹
9 ⁷	5 ³	7 ⁵

MONTH 5 2000
June 2–July 1

5 ⁴	7 ⁶	3 ²
9 ⁸	1 ⁹	2 ¹
8 ⁷	4 ³	6 ⁵

MONTH 6 2000
July 2–July 30

4 ⁴	6 ⁶	2 ²
8 ⁸	9 ⁹	1 ¹
7 ⁷	3 ³	5 ⁵

Education, study and learning
Financial success

Status, credibility and advantage
Career and business

MONTH 7 2000
July 31–August 28

3 ^{4}	5 ^{6}	1 ^{2}
7 ^{8}	🥂 8 ^{9}	9 ^{1}
6 ^{7}	2 ^{3}	4 ^{5}

MONTH 8 2000
August 29–September 27

2 ^{4}	☼ 4 ^{6}	🔲 9 ^{2}
6 ^{8}	7 ^{9}	8 ^{1}
5 ^{7}	1 ^{3}	3 ^{5}

MONTH 9 2000
September 28–October 26

1 ^{4}	3 ^{6}	8 ^{2}
5 ^{8}	6 ^{9}	7 ^{1}
4 ^{7}	9 ^{3}	✚ 2 ^{5}

MONTH 10 2000
October 27–November 25

📅 9 ^{4}	2 ^{6}	👒 7 ^{2} **CAUTION**
4 ^{8}	5 ^{9}	📖 6 ^{1}
3 ^{7} ☀	8 ^{3}	1 ^{5}

MONTH 11 2000
November 26–December 25

8 ^{4}	📖 1 ^{6}	6 ^{2}
🎖 3 ^{8} **VERY GOOD**	📅 4 ^{9}	5 ^{1}
👒 2 ^{7}	7 ^{3}	9 ^{5}

MONTH 12 2000
December 26–January 23

7 ^{4}	9 ^{6}	✚ 5 ^{2}
2 ^{8}	3 ^{9}	4 ^{1}
1 ^{7}	6 ^{3}	8 ^{5}

☼ Fame
🥂 Family harmony and celebration

✚ Sickness
🔲 Problems in business

FLYING STARS FOR 1999

7	3	2
5	1	6
9	8	4

FLYING STARS FOR 2000

6	2	1
4	9	5
8	7	3

PORTENTS

HAI HUO ACCIDENTS	CHUEH MING BROKEN FATE	WU KUEI FIVE GHOSTS
SHENG CHI SOURCE OF CHI	DOOR FACES EAST ↓	T'IEN I HEAVENLY DOCTOR
NIEN YEN LONG LIFE		LIU SHA SIX IMPS

MONTH 10 1999
November 8–December 7

5 ⁷	1 ³	9 ²
3 ⁵	8 ¹	4 ⁶
7 ⁹	6 ⁸	2 ⁴

MONTH 11 1999
December 8–January 6

4 ⁷	9 ³	8 ²
2 ⁵	7 ¹	3 ⁶
6 ⁹	5 ⁸	1 ⁴

MONTH 12 1999
January 7–February 4

3 ⁷	8 ³	7 ² CAUTION
1 ⁵	6 ¹	2 ⁶
5 ⁹	4 ⁸	9 ⁴

Education, study and learning

Financial success

Status, credibility and advantage

Career and business

175

MONTH 1 2000
February 5–March 5

2 [6]	7 [2] 📖	6 [1]
	CAUTION	
👜 9 [4]	5 [9]	1 [5]
4 [8]	3 [7]	🏵 8 [3]

MONTH 2 2000
March 6–April 4

📖 1 [6]	6 [2]	5 [1]
8 [4]	👜 4 [9]	9 [5]
🏵 3 [8]	2 [7]	7 [3]
VERY GOOD		

MONTH 3 2000
April 5–May 3

9 [6]	✚ 5 [2]	4 [1]
7 [4]	3 [9]	8 [5]
2 [8]	1 [7]	6 [3]

MONTH 4 2000
May 4–June 1

8 [6]	4 [2]	3 [1]
☆ 6 [4]	🏚 2 [9]	7 [5]
1 [8]	9 [7]	5 [3]

MONTH 5 2000
June 2–July 1

7 [6]	3 [2]	2 [1]
5 [4]	1 [9]	6 [5]
🍷 9 [8]	8 [7]	4 [3]

MONTH 6 2000
July 2–July 30

6 [6]	2 [2]	1 [1]
4 [4]	9 [9]	5 [5]
8 [8]	7 [7]	3 [3]

☆ Fame

🍷 Family harmony and celebration

176

✚ Sickness

🏚 Problems in business

MONTH 7 2000
July 31–August 28

5 ⁶	1 ²	9 ¹
3 ⁴	🥂 8 ⁹	4 ⁵
7 ⁸	6 ⁷	2 ³

MONTH 8 2000
August 29–September 27

✨ 4 ⁶	🗓 9 ²	8 ¹
2 ⁴	7 ⁹	3 ⁵
6 ⁸	5 ⁷	1 ³

MONTH 9 2000
September 28–October 26

3 ⁶	8 ²	7 ¹
1 ⁴	6 ⁹	✚ 2 ⁵
5 ⁸	4 ⁷	9 ³

MONTH 10 2000
October 27–November 25

2 ⁶	👞 7 ²	📖 6 ¹
	CAUTION	
👜 9 ⁴	5 ⁹	1 ⁵
4 ⁸	3 ⁷	🏵 8 ³

MONTH 11 2000
November 26–December 25

📖 1 ⁶	6 ²	5 ¹
8 ⁴	👜 4 ⁹	9 ⁵
🏵 3 ⁸	👞 2 ⁷	7 ³
VERY GOOD		

MONTH 12 2000
December 26–January 23

9 ⁶	✚ 5 ²	4 ¹
7 ⁴	3 ⁹	8 ⁵
2 ⁸	1 ⁷	6 ³

 Education, study and learning

 Financial success

177

🏵 Status, credibility and advantage

👜 Career and business

FLYING STARS FOR 1999

3	2	6
7	1	4
5	9	8

FLYING STARS FOR 2000

2	1	5
6	9	3
4	8	7

PORTENTS

LIU SHA SIX IMPS	HAI HUO ACCIDENTS	SHENG CHI SOURCE OF CHI
WU KUEI FIVE GHOSTS	DOOR FACES SOUTH EAST ↓	CHUEH MING BROKEN FATE
T'IEN I HEAVENLY DOCTOR		NIEN YEN LONG LIFE

MONTH 10 1999
November 8–December 7

1 ³	9 ² 🧮	4 ⁶ ✨
5 ⁷	8 ¹	2 ⁴
3 ⁵	7 ⁹	6 ⁸

MONTH 11 1999
December 8–January 6

9 ³	8 ²	3 ⁶
4 ⁷	7 ¹	1 ⁴
➕ 2 ⁵	6 ⁹	5 ⁸

MONTH 12 1999
January 7–February 4

🌀 8 ³	🎩 7 ²	2 ⁶
	CAUTION	
3 ⁷	📖 6 ¹	🛍 9 ⁴
1 ⁵	5 ⁹	4 ⁸

✨ Fame

🍾 Family harmony and celebration

➕ Sickness

🧮 Problems in business

178

MONTH 1 2000
February 5–March 5

7 [2] CAUTION	6 [1]	1 [5]
2 [6]	5 [9]	8 [3]
9 [4]	4 [8]	3 [7]

MONTH 2 2000
March 6–April 4

6 [2]	5 [1]	9 [5]
1 [6]	4 [9]	7 [3]
8 [4]	3 [8] VERY GOOD	2 [7]

MONTH 3 2000
April 5–May 3

5 [2]	4 [1]	8 [5]
9 [6]	3 [9]	6 [3]
7 [4]	2 [8]	1 [7]

MONTH 4 2000
May 4–June 1

4 [2]	3 [1]	7 [5]
8 [6]	2 [9]	5 [3]
6 [4]	1 [8]	9 [7]

MONTH 5 2000
June 2–July 1

3 [2]	2 [1]	6 [5]
7 [6]	1 [9]	4 [3]
5 [4]	9 [8]	8 [7]

MONTH 6 2000
July 2–July 30

2 [2]	1 [1]	5 [5]
6 [6]	9 [9]	3 [3]
4 [4]	8 [8]	7 [7]

Education, study and learning

Financial success

Status, credibility and advantage

Career and business

179

MONTH 7 2000
July 31–August 28

1 ²	9 ¹	4 ⁵
5 ⁶	🥂 8 ⁹	2 ³
3 ⁴	7 ⁸	6 ⁷

MONTH 8 2000
August 29–September 27

🀫 9 ²	8 ¹	3 ⁵
☆ 4 ⁶	7 ⁹	1 ³
2 ⁴	6 ⁸	5 ⁷

MONTH 9 2000
September 28–October 26

8 ²	7 ¹	✚ 2 ⁵
3 ⁶	6 ⁹	9 ³
1 ⁴	5 ⁸	4 ⁷

MONTH 10 2000
October 27–November 25

🔧 7 ²	📖 6 ¹	1 ⁵
CAUTION		
2 ⁶	5 ⁹	🐚 8 ³
📅 9 ⁴	4 ⁸	3 ⁷

MONTH 11 2000
November 26–December 25

6 ²	5 ¹	9 ⁵
📖 1 ⁶	📅 4 ⁹	7 ³
8 ⁴	🐚 3 ⁸	2 ⁷
	VERY GOOD	

MONTH 12 2000
December 26–January 23

✚ 5 ²	4 ¹	8 ⁵
9 ⁶	3 ⁹	6 ³
7 ⁴	2 ⁸	1 ⁷

☆ Fame

🥂 Family harmony and celebration

✚ Sickness

🀫 Problems in business

FLYING STARS FOR 1999

2	6	4
3	1	8
7	5	9

FLYING STARS FOR 2000

1	5	3
2	9	7
6	4	8

PORTENTS

CHUEH MING BROKEN FATE	NIEN YEN LONG LIFE	HAI HUO ACCIDENTS
WU KUEI FIVE GHOSTS	DOOR FACES SOUTH ↓	SHENG CHI SOURCE OF CHI
LIU SHA SIX IMPS		T'IEN I HEAVENLY DOCTOR

MONTH 10 1999
November 8–December 7

9 ²	4 ⁶	2 ⁴
1 ³	8 ¹	6 ⁸
5 ⁷	3 ⁵	7 ⁹

MONTH 11 1999
December 8–January 6

8 ²	3 ⁶	1 ⁴
9 ³	7 ¹	5 ⁸
4 ⁷	2 ⁵	6 ⁹

MONTH 12 1999
January 7–February 4

7 ² CAUTION	2 ⁶	9 ⁴
8 ³	6 ¹	4 ⁸
3 ⁷	1 ⁵	5 ⁹

Education, study and learning

Financial success

Status, credibility and advantage

Career and business

MONTH 1 2000
February 5–March 5

6 [1]	1 [5]	8 [3]
7 [2] **CAUTION**	5 [9]	3 [7]
2 [6]	9 [4]	4 [8]

MONTH 2 2000
March 6–April 4

5 [1]	9 [5]	7 [3]
6 [2]	4 [9]	2 [7]
1 [6]	8 [4]	3 [8] **VERY GOOD**

MONTH 3 2000
April 5–May 3

4 [1]	8 [5]	6 [3]
5 [2]	3 [9]	1 [7]
9 [6]	7 [4]	2 [8]

MONTH 4 2000
May 4–June 1

3 [1]	7 [5]	5 [3]
4 [2]	2 [9]	9 [7]
8 [6]	6 [4]	1 [8]

MONTH 5 2000
June 2–July 1

2 [1]	6 [5]	4 [3]
3 [2]	1 [9]	8 [7]
7 [6]	5 [4]	9 [8]

MONTH 6 2000
July 2–July 30

1 [1]	5 [5]	3 [3]
2 [2]	9 [9]	7 [7]
6 [6]	4 [4]	8 [8]

☆ Fame
♉ Family harmony and celebration

✚ Sickness
▦ Problems in business

MONTH 7 2000
July 31–August 28

9 ¹	4 ⁵	2 ³
1 ²	8 ⁹	6 ⁷
5 ⁶	3 ⁴	7 ⁸

MONTH 8 2000
August 29–September 27

8 ¹	3 ⁵	1 ³
9 ²	7 ⁹	5 ⁷
4 ⁶	2 ⁴	6 ⁸

MONTH 9 2000
September 28–October 26

7 ¹	2 ⁵	9 ³
8 ²	6 ⁹	4 ⁷
3 ⁶	1 ⁴	5 ⁸

MONTH 10 2000
October 27–November 25

6 ¹	1 ⁵	8 ³
7 ²	5 ⁹	3 ⁷
CAUTION		
2 ⁶	9 ⁴	4 ⁸

MONTH 11 2000
November 26–December 25

5 ¹	9 ⁵	7 ³
6 ²	4 ⁹	2 ⁷
1 ⁶	8 ⁴	3 ⁸
		VERY GOOD

MONTH 12 2000
December 26–January 23

4 ¹	8 ⁵	6 ³
5 ²	3 ⁹	1 ⁷
9 ⁶	7 ⁴	2 ⁸

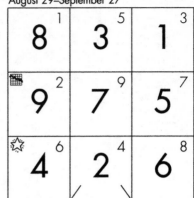

Education, study and learning

Financial success

Status, credibility and advantage

Career and business

183

FLYING STARS FOR 1999

6	4	8
2	1	9
3	7	5

FLYING STARS FOR 2000

5	3	7
1	9	8
2	6	4

PORTENTS

CHUEH MING BROKEN FATE	SHENG CHI SOURCE OF CHI	HAI HUO ACCIDENTS
NIEN YEN LONG LIFE	DOOR FACES SOUTH WEST ↓	WU KUEI FIVE GHOSTS
T'IEN I HEAVENLY DOCTOR		LIU SHA SIX IMPS

MONTH 10 1999
November 8–December 7

☆ 6 4	4	☆ 8
2	2	6
▦ 2	1	9
9	8	7
3	7	5
1	5	3

MONTH 11 1999
December 8–January 6

6	4	8
3	1	5
2	1	9
8	7	6
3	7	5
9	4	✚ 2

MONTH 12 1999
January 7–February 4

6	👜 4	8
2	9	4
🪙 2	📖 1	9
7	6	5
CAUTION		
3	7	5
8	3	1

☆ Fame
👰 Family harmony and celebration
✚ Sickness
▦ Problems in business

MONTH 1 2000
February 5–March 5

1 ⁵	8 ³	3 ⁷
6 ¹	5 ⁹	4 ⁸
7 ² **CAUTION**	2 ⁶	9 ⁴

MONTH 2 2000
March 6–April 4

9 ⁵	7 ³	2 ⁷
5 ¹	4 ⁹	3 ⁸ **VERY GOOD**
6 ²	1 ⁶	8 ⁴

MONTH 3 2000
April 5–May 3

8 ⁵	6 ³	1 ⁷
4 ¹	3 ⁹	2 ⁸
5 ²	9 ⁶	7 ⁴

MONTH 4 2000
May 4–June 1

7 ⁵	5 ³	9 ⁷
3 ¹	2 ⁹	1 ⁸
4 ²	8 ⁶	6 ⁴

MONTH 5 2000
June 2–July 1

6 ⁵	4 ³	8 ⁷
2 ¹	1 ⁹	9 ⁸
3 ²	7 ⁶	5 ⁴

MONTH 6 2000
July 2–July 30

5 ⁵	3 ³	7 ⁷
1 ¹	9 ⁹	8 ⁸
2 ²	6 ⁶	4 ⁴

Education, study and learning

Financial success

Status, credibility and advantage

Career and business

MONTH 7 2000
July 31–August 28

4 ⁵	2 ³	6 ⁷
9 ¹	🥂 8 ⁹	7 ⁸
1 ²	5 ⁶	3 ⁴

MONTH 8 2000
August 29–September 27

3 ⁵	1 ³	5 ⁷
8 ¹	7 ⁹	6 ⁸
🗒 9 ²	☆ 4 ⁶	2 ⁴

MONTH 9 2000
September 28–October 26

✚ 2 ⁵	9 ³	4 ⁷
7 ¹	6 ⁹	5 ⁸
8 ²	3 ⁶	1 ⁴

MONTH 10 2000
October 27–November 25

1 ⁵	🏅 8 ³	3 ⁷
📖 6 ¹	5 ⁹	4 ⁸
👒 7 ²	2 ⁶	🛍 9 ⁴

CAUTION

MONTH 11 2000
November 26–December 25

9 ⁵	7 ³	👒 2 ⁷
5 ¹	🛍 4 ⁹	🏅 3 ⁸
6 ²	📖 1 ⁶	8 ⁴

VERY GOOD

MONTH 12 2000
December 26–January 23

8 ⁵	6 ³	1 ⁷
4 ¹	3 ⁹	2 ⁸
✚ 5 ²	9 ⁶	7 ⁴

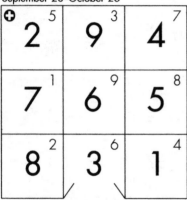

☆ Fame

🥂 Family harmony and celebration

✚ Sickness

🗒 Problems in business

FLYING STARS FOR 1999

4	8	9
6	1	5
2	3	7

FLYING STARS FOR 2000

3	7	8
5	9	4
1	2	6

PORTENTS

NIEN YEN LONG LIFE	**CHUEH MING** BROKEN FATE	**LIU SHA** SIX IMPS
HAI HUO ACCIDENTS	**DOOR FACES WEST** ↓	**WU KUEI** FIVE GHOSTS
SHENG CHI SOURCE OF CHI		**T'IEN I** HEAVENLY DOCTOR

MONTH 10 1999
November 8–December 7

2 ⁴	6 ⁸	7 ⁹
☆ 4 ⁶	8 ¹	3 ⁵
▦ 9 ²	1 ³	5 ⁷

MONTH 11 1999
December 8–January 6

1 ⁴	5 ⁸	6 ⁹
3 ⁶	7 ¹	✛ 2 ⁵
8 ²	9 ³	4 ⁷

MONTH 12 1999
January 7–February 4

📕 9 ⁴	4 ⁸	5 ⁹
2 ⁶	📖 6 ¹	1 ⁵
🎩 7 ²	⚙ 8 ³	3 ⁷
CAUTION		

 Education, study and learning

Financial success

Status, credibility and advantage

Career and business

MONTH 1 2000
February 5–March 5

🏵 8 ³	3 ⁷	4 ⁸
1 ⁵	5 ⁹	🛍 9 ⁴
📖 6 ¹	👒 7 ² /CAUTION\	2 ⁶

MONTH 2 2000
March 6–April 4

7 ³	👒 2 ⁷	🏵 3 ⁸ VERY GOOD
9 ⁵	🛍 4 ⁹	8 ⁴
5 ¹	6 ²	📖 1 ⁶

MONTH 3 2000
April 5–May 3

6 ³	1 ⁷	2 ⁸
8 ⁵	3 ⁹	7 ⁴
4 ¹	➕ 5 ²	9 ⁶

MONTH 4 2000
May 4–June 1

5 ³	9 ⁷	1 ⁸
7 ⁵	🏢 2 ⁹	☆ 6 ⁴
3 ¹	4 ²	8 ⁶

MONTH 5 2000
June 2–July 1

4 ³	8 ⁷	🥂 9 ⁸
6 ⁵	1 ⁹	5 ⁴
2 ¹	3 ²	7 ⁶

MONTH 6 2000
July 2–July 30

3 ³	7 ⁷	8 ⁸
5 ⁵	9 ⁹	4 ⁴
1 ¹	2 ²	6 ⁶

☆ Fame
🥂 Family harmony and celebration

➕ Sickness
🏢 Problems in business

188

MONTH 7 2000
July 31–August 28

2 ³	6 ⁷	7 ⁸
4 ⁵	🥂 8 ⁹	3 ⁴
9 ¹	1 ²	5 ⁶

MONTH 8 2000
August 29–September 27

1 ³	5 ⁷	6 ⁸
3 ⁵	7 ⁹	2 ⁴
8 ¹	🀫 9 ²	☆ 4 ⁶

MONTH 9 2000
September 28–October 26

9 ³	4 ⁷	5 ⁸
✚ 2 ⁵	6 ⁹	1 ⁴
7 ¹	8 ²	3 ⁶

MONTH 10 2000
October 27–November 25

🏵 8 ³	3 ⁷	4 ⁸
1 ⁵	5 ⁹	👜 9 ⁴
📖 6 ¹	👞 7 ²	2 ⁶

CAUTION

MONTH 11 2000
November 26–December 25

7 ³	👞 2 ⁷	🏵 3 ⁸
		VERY GOOD
9 ⁵	👜 4 ⁹	8 ⁴
5 ¹	6 ²	📖 1 ⁶

MONTH 12 2000
December 26–January 23

6 ³	1 ⁷	2 ⁸
8 ⁵	3 ⁹	7 ⁴
4 ¹	✚ 5 ²	9 ⁶

📖 Education, study and learning

👞 Financial success

🏵 Status, credibility and advantage

👜 Career and business

FLYING STARS FOR 1999

8	9	5
4	1	7
6	2	3

FLYING STARS FOR 2000

7	8	4
3	9	6
5	1	2

PORTENTS

WU KUEI FIVE GHOSTS	**HAI HUO** ACCIDENTS	**CHUEH MING** BROKEN FATE
T'IEN I HEAVENLY DOCTOR	**DOOR FACES NORTH WEST** ↓	**NIEN YEN** LONG LIFE
LIU SHA SIX IMPS		**SHENG CHI** SOURCE OF CHI

MONTH 10 1999
November 8–December 7

6 ⁸	7 ⁹	3 ⁵
2 ⁴	8 ¹	5 ⁷
☆ 4 ⁶	▦ 9 ²	1 ³

MONTH 11 1999
December 8–January 6

5 ⁸	6 ⁹	✚ 2 ⁵
1 ⁴	7 ¹	4 ⁷
3 ⁶	8 ²	9 ³

MONTH 12 1999
January 7–February 4

4 ⁸	5 ⁹	1 ⁵
9 ⁴	6 ¹	3 ⁷
2 ⁶	7 ²	8 ³

CAUTION

 Fame

Family harmony and celebration

 Sickness

Problems in business

MONTH 1 2000
February 5–March 5

3 ⁷	4 ⁸	👜 9 ⁴
🏵 8 ³	5 ⁹	2 ⁶
1 ⁵	📖 6 ¹	🎩 7 ² **CAUTION**

MONTH 2 2000
March 6–April 4

🎩 2 ⁷	🏵 3 ⁸ **VERY GOOD**	8 ⁴
7 ³	👜 4 ⁹	📖 1 ⁶
9 ⁵	5 ¹	6 ²

MONTH 3 2000
April 5–May 3

1 ⁷	2 ⁸	7 ⁴
6 ³	3 ⁹	9 ⁶
8 ⁵	4 ¹	➕ 5 ²

MONTH 4 2000
May 4–June 1

9 ⁷	1 ⁸	✨ 6 ⁴
5 ³	🏠 2 ⁹	8 ⁶
7 ⁵	3 ¹	4 ²

MONTH 5 2000
June 2–July 1

8 ⁷	🥂 9 ⁸	5 ⁴
4 ³	1 ⁹	7 ⁶
6 ⁵	2 ¹	3 ²

MONTH 6 2000
July 2–July 30

7 ⁷	8 ⁸	4 ⁴
3 ³	9 ⁹	6 ⁶
5 ⁵	1 ¹	2 ²

📖 Education, study and learning

💰 Financial success

🏵 Status, credibility and advantage

👜 Career and business

MONTH 7 2000
July 31–August 28

6 ⁷	7 ⁸	3 ⁴
2 ³	🥂 8 ⁹	5 ⁶
4 ⁵	9 ¹	1 ²

MONTH 8 2000
August 29–September 27

5 ⁷	6 ⁸	2 ⁴
1 ³	7 ⁹	✨ 4 ⁶
3 ⁵	8 ¹	▦ 9 ²

MONTH 9 2000
September 28–October 26

4 ⁷	5 ⁸	1 ⁴
9 ³	6 ⁹	3 ⁶
✛ 2 ⁵	7 ¹	8 ²

MONTH 10 2000
October 27–November 25

3 ⁷	4 ⁸	🛍 9 ⁴
🏵 8 ³	5 ⁹	2 ⁶
1 ⁵	📖 6 ¹	👡 7 ² **CAUTION**

MONTH 11 2000
November 26–December 25

👡 2 ⁷	🏵 3 ⁸ **VERY GOOD**	8 ⁴
7 ³	🛍 4 ⁹	📖 1 ⁶
9 ⁵	5 ¹	6 ²

MONTH 12 2000
December 26–January 23

1 ⁷	2 ⁸	7 ⁴
6 ³	3 ⁹	9 ⁶
8 ⁵	4 ¹	✛ 5 ²

✨ Fame

🥂 Family harmony and celebration

✛ Sickness

▦ Problems in business